MW01100674

If you or someone you care about is struggling with any kind of emotional distress, call or text 988. The National Suicide and Crisis Hotline is staffed 24/7 with trained counselors available to talk, text, or chat.

Also by Nancy Casey

All the Way to Second Street
This is Mega-Mathematics (with Michael R. Fellows)
The View from Planet Nancy (podcast)
Write for You (blog, Latah Recovery Center)

Raised by God

The Autobiography of
Patricia Clayton

Nancy Casey

Logwood Stone
Moscow, Idaho

Casey, Nancy

Raised by God: The Autobiography of Patricia Clayton

BIOGRAPHY AND AUTOBIOGRAPHY/Women
ADDICTION/Narcotics—Relationships—Recovery
FAMILY/Abuse—Intergenerational Trauma
RELIGION/Spirituality—Christianity
SPOKANE, WA/History 1960-2000

ISBN 978-1-937203-02-3

Cover Image: StreetWill.co
Cover Background: via Canva
Patricia Clayton photo: Sheryl

Raised by God

The Autobiography of Patricia Clayton

For my children

My story is my most precious possession.

Table of Contents

1. The Faith of a Troubled Child 9

2. Love and Marriage 35

3. A Man Who Will Protect Me 65

4. Downward Spiral 107

5. Drug House 153

6. Recovery 167

7. The City of Contentment 197

Acknowledgements 202

Author's Note.. 204

1. The Faith of a Troubled Child

I was born in 1956. My earliest memory is of my fingertips, watching them poke through the holes in a lace tablecloth that draped down from the little table I was sitting under, near Mama's feet. In the living room, my aunt and uncle were shouting and throwing things. Aunts and uncles got in fights all the time. Far more interesting to me was the way the holes would stretch when I squeezed another finger alongside the first. Mama reached down and slapped me again and again, telling me to quit being so *bad*. I remember being scolded in the car on the way home and not understanding why. I didn't know what *bad* was, much less how to stop being that way. *Bad* was what made me and everything I did permanently wrong somehow.

Mama was capable and wise. I admired her so much. Every summer she put up tomatoes, peaches, pickles, and jam. She ruled the kitchen at big family gatherings. I listened for hours as she talked on the phone, explaining the conflicts and drama between my many relatives, declaring who should apologize to whom and why. Decades would go by before I'd realize how much she reveled in gossip, and how much of what she said was exaggerated or untrue.

I was, as she always said, a sickly child. *Anemia* was the thing I was born with that made me that way. Later she changed it to *leukemia,* a special kind that some children outgrow. Did the doctor really tell her not to get attached to me because I wasn't going to live very long? According to Mama, the doctor said she should put her efforts into getting pregnant again and carrying a healthy child to term. My brother came along a year after I did. Meanwhile, instead of dying, I screamed. Day and night.

Mama was so exhausted by my crying that she feared she would miscarry the healthy baby. Since I wasn't going to live much longer anyway, she shut me into a dark room, hoping I would just scream myself to death and get it over with. But the plan never worked. When her milk came down, it was so painful she was forced to fetch me and allow me to nurse.

When I got a little older and we had guests, she would introduce my elder sister and younger brother first, praising them and telling stories about their accomplishments. Then she would call me to her side, hold me close, and say, "This is Trish, our middle child, the one we have to explain." In her entertaining stories I was always sickly and dumb. She sighed over the fact that I still wet the bed and wagged her head sadly about how I would succumb to my ailments before my 12th birthday. I believed I was that ill. The bedwetting alone proved there was something terribly wrong with me.

Back then, bill collectors came right to your house, and apparently my parents had a lot of bills. When the doorbell rang, Mama called me to her side. I leaned against her in my sickly way while she stroked my head and explained to the man on the porch how terribly ill I was and didn't have many years to live. The man would apologize for disturbing us and often make generous concessions.

My bedroom was in the basement. I could lie in bed and listen to conversations going on upstairs through a heating duct. One night I heard my parents arguing about me, Daddy blaming Mama for the way I was.

"Well then what do you want me to do with her?" she demanded. "Put her up for adoption?"

I feared that any day they might send me away. I had no idea what I could do to prevent it.

Next to my bedroom was a rec room with a couch and a TV. There, I snuggled my white tomcat SnoBall and watched the families on television. Soap operas appealed to me because I identified with all the emotional pain and the ways people were mean and deceived one another. Westerns were the best, always starring handsome cowboys dedicated to righting wrongs. I adored the men on *Bonanza*. Ben Cartwright was a gentle, perfect father, and Hoss the ideal big brother. Little Joe was a bit silly, always smitten with one lady or another. Someday I would marry someone like Adam—tall, dark-haired, polite, and always knowing the right thing to do. When I got a little older, I fantasized that I was married to Captain Kirk and together we shared love and adventures all over the universe.

Daddy got angry a lot. The few details I know of his childhood were the ones recounted by Mama. His mother had six or eight children, then her husband died. She married his brother and had another six or eight kids with him. Daddy was the youngest. I had all kinds of uncles, aunts, and cousins living in Spokane, Washington, and the surrounding area, most of whom were drunks, addicts, or otherwise dysfunctional. Mama said they all treated him, the baby, terribly.

Daddy drove a truck for a warehouse and made deliveries all around Spokane. Us kids were usually down in the basement watching TV when he got home from work. When his headlights shone into the high basement window, we fell silent, listening to see what kind of mood he was in. If he came into the house singing "Happy Birthday to Me," we were safe, provided Mama didn't have issues with one of us that day. If she did, she sat in a chair right by the door, ready to deliver the news of our bad behavior as soon as he walked in. If there was no singing, or if the song stopped abruptly, we stayed downstairs in the futile hope that we wouldn't be called up for dinner.

At our house, dinnertime never unfolded the way it did on *The Waltons*. Mama ate dinner in her chair in the living room. Us kids sat at the table with Daddy who always began a "conversation." He considered himself far more educated and knowledgeable than he was. There was no telling what topic he might launch into, but eventually something about the way we responded always set him off. Once, he insisted that the American Bald Eagle got its name because it was indeed bald. We thought he was joking. He made us look it up. When the encyclopedia proved him wrong, he exploded into a rage so big, I have blotted the details of what happened next from my mind.

Daddy's favorite blow was an open-handed smack upside the head. Teachers didn't look as closely at children's bruises as they do today. Kids played rough. They wrestled, got hit with fly balls and wrecked their bikes. A black eye was a trophy among children and nothing adults questioned very much. Daddy liked spankings, too. A spanking was license to turn a kid over and hit them as hard as you could until you were spent. One summer day when I was playing I the yard under the elm tree, my sister burst out of the house and ran across the lawn with Daddy in close pursuit. She must have been about sixteen. He tackled her, football style, held her down, and pummeled her. I never found out what set him off that time.

My bedroom was cold in winter and infested with spiders. Even so, it was the only place in the house I felt safe. The spiders came out in the dark. I listened to the quiet *plops* as they fell off the ceiling. Even my pillow was not off limits for them. When I figured out that they didn't like the light, I shone my desk lamp onto the bed and could sleep. Finding a dry place to sleep was not as easy.

I peed the bed every night until I gave birth to my first child. I tried everything to keep myself from wetting the bed—sleeping sideways with my feet hanging off, setting an alarm to get up and pee at midnight, but nothing worked. Daddy, convinced that my bed wetting was intentional, reacted with fury. I was only permitted to change my bedding, take a bath, and put on clean pajamas once a week, so going to sleep always started in disappointment and shame. I folded my blanket in different ways each night, trying to make a dry spot. By the end of the week, my bed and bedding were always soaked through to the mattress. I hated myself for these failures.

It was when I was curled up in bed, often crying, squeezing myself into a dry spot, wishing someone would love me, that I made friends with God.

Nobody in my house ever talked about God, but Mama took us to church, so I learned about Him in Sunday School. He loved me. I learned about Jesus, who was kind and loved children. He never did anything wrong, yet He was bullied and reviled by people he loved. Even then, He did not strike back in anger. I believed that God was my friend. When I couldn't sleep, I would cry and pray, sometimes for hours. I loved God and felt God's love for me. I asked God to send a person to love me. I would love them back.

When I say "God" I don't picture a white-bearded man who tallies people's sins. In my bedroom, God was a presence I could feel high in one corner of the room. When I talked to Him in my mind, the presence became stronger. A gentle voice came into my thoughts from that corner. It reassured me, told me that I was a valuable person, and that this horrible loneliness wasn't going to last forever. Sometimes there were angels who spoke, too. Their leader was a male warrior named Acceptance. A female angel named Serenity came as well, along with twins named Patience and Tolerance. They stood beside me and whispered in my ear. These and other angels remain with me today, offering comfort and guidance.

My life has been difficult, painful, and confusing. I have done so many things that I am ashamed of. I have been furious with God and called Him terrible names. I have been confused about how God works in my life. But I have always felt this presence. In my childhood bed I told God that He didn't understand how hard it was to live without a single person, someone everyone could see, who loved you. I believed he answered by sending me SnoBall and Angie Farrell.

SnoBall was a pure white tomcat who wandered into my life in first grade. I don't know where he came from, but he knew he was mine. I was responsible for the chickens at that time. The chicken house became a refuge where I could be away from my family. I spent whole evenings there, any weather, any time of year. SnoBall always joined me. I sat still and rattled the nests. SnoBall ran behind them. If there was a mouse back there, I would hear the *crunch-crunch* of him devouring his feast.

Daddy hated SnoBall, and vice-versa. Even when SnoBall sprayed the furniture right in front of Daddy, he refused to get him neutered. Instead he kicked him whenever he saw him, but SnoBall was too fast. When we weren't in the chicken house, SnoBall hid with me in my room.

Many nights after I fled to my bed in tears, SnoBall licked my cheeks and purred. He slept under the covers every night regardless of their condition. At the end of the school day, I called his name from four blocks away. He came running to meet me and walk me home. He was the only reason I liked being in my house.

One day I did something wrong. I don't remember what it was—people were always telling me I was doing something wrong. Daddy decided that to punish me he would punish my SnoBall. It was the middle of winter, cold and snowy. To teach me a lesson, Daddy said SnoBall had to stay outside for four days. My poor freezing kitty meowed and clawed at the basement window trying to find a way in. I cried in my bed, knowing I was failing my only friend, wondering why I didn't have the strength to defy my father and let him inside. Was this weakness what made me *bad?*

I was drawn to Angie Farrell from the moment she joined our class in second grade. She was different. Nobody wanted to sit near her. She had some kind of spinal disability and wore a body cast. I moved my seat to be next to her. The bullies who picked on me murmured in delight at their new target. Our similarities made us the best of friends.

My time with Angie was the most freedom I had ever known in my life. She lived across from the school. I would fly home after class and scurry through my chores. I smoothed over the mess in my room and tossed some feed to the chickens. Mama was in bed at the time with a badly broken leg and it was my job to help her. I emptied her bed pan, brought her a snack, and then ran the five blocks back to Angie's house as fast as I could. Her mother was always smiling, always happy to see me.

We shared a love of music. Angie was learning to play the piano. We sang all the songs from *Mary Poppins* and *The Sound of Music*. My favorite song of all was *The Green Beret*. If Angie didn't know a song, we learned it together. The thing I remember most besides the singing was how much we laughed. The Farrells told stories that were funny without being mean. Angie was the first friend I had ever had and vice-versa. At school, the mean words of the bullies affected us less because we had each other. I never felt such love and connection with a person before.

Angie was sick, though, and in the hospital a lot. When that happened, I was sad and missed her terribly. She had surgery after surgery and was in a lot of pain. Her mother would call Mama and tell her how much Angie wanted me to visit her. Sometimes Mama would give in and allow Mrs. Farrell to come and take me to her. Back then children were considered germ-carriers and not allowed in hospitals, so we had to get creative. Once, I climbed a ladder to a hospital window where the nurses had kindly rolled Angie's bed from down the hall so we could visit. It was just for a few minutes, but it meant the world to us.

Between visits, I was sustained by the knowledge that Angie loved me. She never cared how I smelled. She worried about me. Once, I had a bad case of eczema between my legs from the urine. It hurt a lot, but only Angie knew. She lifted my skirt in front of Mama to show her the awful rash. Mama shushed her and pushed her away. Though I was embarrassed, I was grateful. Nobody had ever stood up for me like that.

Anyone could see how much I loved Angie Farrell. No one told me she was dying.

On a day when Angie was in the hospital, the bullies at school called me over behind a tree and told me she was dead. I was furious at their cruel sneering manner, a meanness worse than what I knew from my own family. Those kids did not even have the right to say her name. Of course I didn't believe them.

At home, Mama said it wasn't true.

The next day at recess the bullies called me back behind the same tree. This time they had a newspaper clipping proving that Angie had died. They laughed and mocked me. Time stopped. I went numb. I grabbed the clipping, ran home, and threw myself on Mama sobbing.

"This is why we didn't want you to know," she said, sounding annoyed by my outburst.

I felt betrayed, and more unloved than ever.

After much protest from Mama, and insistence by Angie's mother, I was allowed to go to Angie's funeral. I was inconsolable. Not that anyone tried to console me. My crying infuriated Mama. I was alone again in a world where not a single person loved me.

The cemetery where they buried Angie was on the way from our house to just about everywhere we went. When we drove past it, I always asked Mama where Angie's grave was and if we could go see her. Finally, I was ordered to stop talking about her. Every time we went to the store, to the doctor, to church, or to a relative's house, I would stare out the window as the car flew past the cemetery, scanning the tombstones for some sign of my friend. My twelfth birthday was years away. It would be a long time before I would be joining her there.

About a year after Angie died, SnoBall got sick. He didn't want to play anymore or even go out to the chicken house. I begged my parents to take him to the vet, but they just shrugged it off and told me he was tired. I knew it was more frightening than that.

Finally, one of my aunts drove me and SnoBall to the vet, a man who was very grouchy. Maybe because I was a shabby little girl who smelled like pee. Maybe because SnoBall was so sick. He showed me SnoBall's gums, and told me they should be pink, not white.

"Anemia," he said.

I knew that word. It means you are going to die.

I threw myself on SnoBall, wailed, and begged for his life. My aunt said that if I loved him, I would let him go. The vet agreed. How could I win an argument like that? I went home alone. My last friend was gone.

I understand now that my sister and brother used me to fend off their own pain about our upbringing. I never expected any affection from my sister. She was four years older and often stuck babysitting my brother and me. We were annoyances to her. Because he was just a year younger than I was, my brother and I sometimes shared adventures, especially in the summer months when we were banished from the house while Mama was canning. He grabbed his Tonka trucks and I my Tammy dolls and we met under the elm tree in the back yard. (No Barbies allowed in our house! They were too shapely, Daddy said. They were sinful and would cause his daughters to turn out like his sisters. I didn't know what that meant.)

My brother seemed to enjoy my company and the adventures we shared with Tammies and trucks. But when things got scary, he forgot the fun we had and looked out only for himself. Whenever he got in trouble, he would find a way to twist the story and blame me. Daddy always believed him. I got the beating. I knew where I stood with my sister, but I thought my brother was my friend and couldn't understand why he did that.

One summer, when I was about ten, my parents worked hard remodeling the house. The kitchen had just been painstakingly painted yellow and white. We had strict orders not to touch anything in the kitchen because of the new paint, with severe threats of what would happen to us if we did. I believed him. He was usually true to his word on matters such as these. I didn't plan to do wrong.

I had just taken a butter knife out of the silverware drawer when time stopped. Knowing the consequences, I carved a line into the front of the drawer with the knife. The paint was thick and still soft. As I watched it give way under the knife, I felt strong, not powerless like I usually did. I made another cut, and then another. Soon the front of the drawer was covered in knife cuts. There was no taking it back. I knew I was going to get beaten.

Daddy saw the drawer immediately when he got home and bellowed for us kids to come up from the basement. He started with my sister. She denied the crime, of course, and was subsequently beaten. She fought back hard. I enjoyed watching her learn how it felt to be punished for something when she was truly innocent. Then it was my brother's turn. I said nothing while he got his spanking. The idea, of course, was that the culprit would speak up rather than watch a sibling get wrongly punished. I liked what I saw and felt nothing.

When it came to my turn and Daddy asked if I had done it, I shamelessly and courageously said yes. Daddy was shocked.

"You did this?"

I repeated my answer, just as fiercely.

"Why did you stand there and let me spank your sister and brother for it?" He must have actually wanted an answer because he was asking, not beating.

"Because they are always blaming me for things they do. I wanted to know what it felt like to watch them get the blame instead."

I think my father believed me. The look on his face went from rage to sadness. I still got my spanking. It was worth it.

On my 12th birthday, I was surprised to wake up alive. The family was scheduled to depart that day for a long camping trip to the Olympic Rain Forest, but I knew my death was near. I had terrible pains in my belly and was bleeding into my underpants. I told Mama, expecting comfort, but she was furious, upset because my father would "find out." The bloody mess, the painful cramping, and my immanent death were apparently going to ruin the camping trip. My sister laughed and mocked me. I didn't know what I was dying of, but Mama had said it would happen, and now it was.

Mama told me to get up in the back of the camper rented for the occasion and be quiet. I begged my sister to tell me what was wrong. She shrieked with laughter, drunk on the whole joke—me getting in trouble and being stupid besides. When the preparations were finished and the camper pulled away, heading for the freeway, I was still losing blood. My shorts and thighs were sticky with it. Panicked, I banged on the window between the cab and the camper, crying hysterically for someone to save me. Daddy was having a hard time maneuvering the large, unfamiliar vehicle into a ferocious wind. He angrily pulled the camper to the shoulder and ordered Mama to go back there and shut me up, which she did, not with explanations or reassurance, but with yelling and threats.

What a way to spend my last day alive, I remember thinking. Later that evening, when we settled in at the campground, Mama came to me secretly with a bra and pads and told me never to tell Daddy about any of this. It would just make him angry, and I had caused enough trouble already.

Angie Farrell was gone. So was SnoBall. I made it past my twelfth birthday. Every morning I still woke up to the shame and disappointment of a wet bed. I stayed home from school with horrible pains every month, but Daddy just accused me of faking. My parents were gone a lot and my sister babysat for my brother and me more and more. I felt like I had three parents and they all hated me. I had no friends at school. I cried in my bed every night, trying to pray, asking God to send someone or something to love me, even though I was so awful.

I had one aunt who was kind, but she lived Tonasket, Washington, nearly a day's drive away. One day she visited and promised me I could pick out one of the puppies from her poodle's litter. It would be mine as soon as it was old enough. I had to wait six weeks. Would she change her mind? Was this a trick? Why was she being so kind to me?

When the puppies were big enough, Mama drove me all the way up to her home. I picked out the whitest one and named him SnoFlake. He licked my face the entire way back to Spokane.

This little puppy was so smart. He loved pleasing people, and soon learned how he could make people laugh, which he enjoyed even more. I taught him loads of tricks, but the best trick of all was that he loved me. He followed me everywhere and slept with me at night. Like SnoBall, he didn't mind the smelly bed. He absorbed my sadness and licked the tears off my cheeks. I called him SnoFee.

Mama always wanted him to perform for company, but he would only perform for me. Instead of enduring my humiliating presentation as "the one we have to explain," I was sent to "go get that dog."

I taught SnoFee to fetch my shoes. I had many pairs. He knew what I meant when I said "tennies" or "black ones" or "boots" and he brought me the ones I asked for. He would trot all the way to the basement, into my room and into the closet, grab a shoe, carry it upstairs, drop it in front of me, then return for the other. Somehow, he figured out on his own that making people laugh was a good thing. People always laughed if he brought the wrong shoe, so he started doing that. When I shook my head, he took it back downstairs and returned with the correct one. He was hilarious.

There was a summer program in the park for kids. SnoFee was popular, so I was liked. I went every weekday and learned to twirl a baton. I became the group leader and invented routines to teach the smaller children. We competed in contests and often won.

At the end of the summer, SnoFee competed at the county pet fair. I put him through his best tricks. As a finale, I made a pile of pinecones, marked one of them and let him smell it. Then I had him sit up with his back to me while I hid the marked pinecone in the pile. When I told him to go find it, he always did. Somehow, he figured out that if he turned his head and peeked, the audience went wild. So we made that part of the act. He won the blue ribbon every year.

All the kids at the summer program adored SnoFee. They bragged about the ribbons he won as if he was their dog, too. I drank in the approval. I was still an outcast at home. When school started, I was an outcast there again, too. In my basement room, I thanked God for sending me SnoFee and for the summers of fun and acceptance.

"Please," I asked Him, "Can't you just send me a person, someone everyone can see, who will love me all the time?" Then, realizing He had already done that once, I would ask for someone who didn't die the way Angie did.

The bed-wetting was so humiliating. I don't know why it continued for so long, or why it stopped when I gave birth to my first baby at age 19.

I think I was about 13, downstairs in my basement room, pretending to be Olivia Newton-John, dancing, singing, and imagining myself as a performer on a stage, while all the imaginary people who watched glowed with appreciation for my talent and good looks. Suddenly, the door opened, and my father stepped in without knocking. Nobody ever did that. I lost my balance and fell backward onto the bed, shocked to be confronted by the person I was escaping from. He scanned my room, searching for an infraction. I felt violated and afraid of what might happen next.

He spotted his chance. It was the middle of the week, and I was wearing clean pajamas. He pounced.

"Are those clean pajamas?"

I raced through my mind, trying to come up with a defense, but could only squeak out a meek little "Yes."

"Where are the ones you should be wearing?"

"In my drawer."

"Then put them on," he roared.

He stood blocking the doorway and watched me dig into the top drawer of my dresser for my dirty, urine-soaked pajamas. I shamefully peeled off the clean ones, and put on the damp, smelly ones. It all happened in slow motion. The woman I was pretending to be on the stage was long gone, along with the idea that I could be beautiful. I was on quite a different stage now. I could tell he was examining my breasts, which were just beginning to form. There was disgust and anger on his face. I buttoned all the buttons on my filthy, wrinkled pajamas. When I was finished, he uttered a threat about how that had better never happen again, turned, and walked away, leaving the door open. The shame was all-consuming.

The safety of my room was shattered. Ever after, when I was alone there, I was aware of the door, wondering who was out there watching me through the cracks, ready to humiliate me as I pretended to be beautiful.

To go to junior high, I had to take a bus. On the first day, I was a turmoil of knots. I still had no friends. As the bus rolled through the route, I tried to collect myself so no one would see how scared I was. I focused on my lap so when they started up the jokes about why I was sitting alone, I could pretend not to hear. When there weren't any other seats left, Mary Tate got on.

We both rode in silence for a bit, while the noisy, obnoxious fun went on all around us.

She spoke first. By the time we got to the school, we were fast friends.

Mary had a hearing deficiency. I learned to gesture as I spoke so I could get my point across. If she didn't follow, she shook her head and touched her ears. I'd find a different way to say it. It was fun to learn to communicate so well.

We did everything together and would often check in during the day at school, because we were both prey to bullies. No bully could bother us when we were together. Now I ran to Mary 's house, SnoFee at my side, as soon as my after-school chores were done. I loved it there.

Despite her hearing problem, Mary played the piano, and of course, we sang. We sang many of the same songs that I sang with Angie. We brought music from choir and girls' chorus home from school and learned it. At the Tate's, people treasured each other and were kind. They talked about current affairs, music, and TV shows. They asked me what I thought.

At school, we picked up a few other unpopular girls and became a group. The jocks named us "The Dogs." We joined up with the Jesus Freaks who sat on the floor in the hallway singing uplifting songs. My favorite was "Pass It On," a song that compares God's love to a spark that starts a fire and warms everyone. A song is like that, too. One person starts it, like a spark. People join in and the song takes hold. I could feel the soothing presence of God as if it was the warmth of a fire when I sang with people like that.

I joined a group called Campus Life and for the first time I experienced a sense of belonging. We went to meetings, song fests, and campouts. We orchestrated adventures like scavenger hunts and wild goose chases. All the girls would pile into my car to cruise East Sprague and the A&W parking lot, every car blasting KJRB. One night we had a valley-wide chase with a car full of basketball players. The guys in the back seat mooned us. We laughed so hard I could hardly drive. I'd never had this kind of fun.

In addition to the music, the conversations, and the laughter, Mary and I spent hours riding horses. Her horse, Robb II, was a palomino stallion and an obedient saddle horse. The Tates also boarded a bay mare named Ginger which I rode.

One day, I noticed a boy standing near the fence, watching us ride. I galloped Ginger over and we talked a little. His name was Lonnie Martin. He was in my math class. He was a Dog, too.

The next morning, Lonnie showed up at my bus stop and handed me a note, asking me to the dance that Friday. I accepted and went to my first dance ever with a boy. I got caught up in the magic of the lights and music. After all my closed-door dance practice in my room, it was liberating to dance without feeling ashamed or lonely.

The next week in math class, Lonnie passed me a note thanking me for coming to the dance with him and asking me to go steady. I sent him a note right back saying yes. Almost all of our communication was

29

in notes. He would write, "I love, love, love you," and I would answer "I love, love, love, love you." By the end of math class, we would have filled the paper with love, love, love. Imagine that! Somebody who loved me. Every morning he walked to my bus stop, and we stood together in silence. We never kissed or even held hands. The only time we ever touched was slow dancing.

In our senior year, Mary had a 4.0 grade point average and mine was 3.0. She said I didn't study enough. We argued.

I studied hard. I really did. But I felt that Mr. Bronson, my history teacher for all six years, gave me Cs no matter how hard I tried. I got high marks on tests, but only average grades on my papers, even though I researched them for hours. Mary didn't believe this. So I set out to prove it to her, and to myself.

I told Mr. Bronson that I was tired of receiving average grades from him, because I learned more from his classes than in any other. He said I got average grades because I was an average student. So I threatened him. If he gave me another C, I promised that I would cry for the entire hour of his class.

At the end of the quarter when I received my C, I crossed my arms, put my head down, and began to cry. It wasn't hard. My friendship with Mary was in jeopardy. My father, who I wanted to show that I was worth something, either ignored or belittled me. I thought about how loving friends like Angie and SnoBall were snatched from me. The life that stretched in front of me promised only loneliness. I never got approval, no matter how hard I tried. I didn't care about crying in front of everyone in the class. They never saw me anyway.

Mr. Bronson thought I was faking it. I was used to that too and shut out his comments to let the tears flow. For the entire hour. After class, Mr. Bronson called me up to his desk to explain my grade. He said my work averaged out to either a B- or a C+, but since he didn't give plusses or minuses, he gave me the C.

One quarter remained before high school graduation. I glared at Mr. Bronson through the entire hour of his class, never taking a single note. I didn't research the assignments and completed tests solely on what I happened to remember. He asked me about the change once. I told him there was no sense in trying when it served no purpose.

At the end of the school year when I got my grades, beside the word "History" was a B. That put me on the Honor Roll. My name was in the paper. I showed my family. They didn't care. It had always been such a big deal when my sister made the Honor Roll. When I asked Mr. Bronson about my grade, he said I had earned it, and besides, he didn't want any more tears in his classroom.

I started to cry.

It was a summer night, just before high school graduation. It must have been late because it was dark. My father asked me to go outside on the porch so we could have a talk. I had no idea what was going to happen. Daddy wanted to talk to me? He never even wanted to see me, let alone have a conversation with me.

I was apprehensive, worrying over what I had done, or not done. He had me sit on a step and he sat on the top landing of the porch. It was an ordinary cement porch. Behind Daddy was a turquoise fiber-glass wall he had put up. It held shelves with garden tools and gloves.

His voice was gentle and sincere, nothing like I had ever heard from him before. He explained that there was something I needed to know that would keep me from disappointment and pain through my life. I sat there, looking up, amazed at this new side of him that I had never seen before. He explained that there were some people in the world who were just not capable of accomplishing anything. I was one of them.

He warned me not to make any plans. College would be wasted on me. Any career choice that I tried to make would be useless. He said that anything I set out to do would end in failure so I should not even try. I had no possibilities, no talents.

For the next several hours into the night, he gently and systematically destroyed all my dreams. I wanted to be a police officer and had even spoken with the counselors at school to make sure I took the right classes during my senior year. They helped me sign up for a program where I could work my way through college. Up until that moment, I was excited about my plans and encouraged for my future away from my family.

I tried to argue back. I told him about my plans. He responded that he knew me better than any teacher could and assured me that anything I tried was destined to end up in failure. When I told him I could do lots of things, he said I was not good enough at anything to ever be able to keep a job.

"But I can clip dogs," I said meekly.

"If you are so good at clipping dogs, where are all the people coming around to have you do it?"

He promised me that I'd never be a good mother or a good wife. The closest thing I had to talent was singing, but I was definitely not good enough at that to be successful. I was a nothing and a nobody, and always would be. He told me he was trying to protect me from being hurt. The only way to spare myself the inevitable pain of failure was to face the fact that I shouldn't even try.

"Please," he said.

I believed him.

I wasted no time moving out of that house after high school. As I stepped into adulthood, my outer confidence was growing. I found I had a knack for making people laugh which led me to make friends and have fun. When a task needed to be done, I could knuckle down, organize the steps, and get it finished. I had experienced God's presence, his love and comfort. This love flowing through me made me compassionate towards others, people and animals alike.

What I did not grasp was that I had a black hole in my heart, a dark, terrible place that beckoned me always. The pain, fear, and rejection I experienced and couldn't express were shoved down there, making a dense core of despair connected to the word *bad*. When events drew me too close to the edge of that black hole it sucked me in. My mind would be so overcome with shame and rage that rational thought was not available to me. Many years went by before I understood this about myself. On my own for the first time, I used the sweet delirium of falling in love to protect me from the well of self-loathing in my heart.

2. Love and Marriage

My first apartment was a converted garage in Mead, about 15 minutes north of Spokane. Nurse's aides were in demand, so I took the course, got certified, and began working nights at a retirement center while taking courses in law enforcement during the day.

There were lots of people my age in Mead. I became fast friends with Lisa Wilson, a girl my age who lived at home, even though her alcoholic father abused her. Her boyfriend was in a program down in Medical Lake, confined to a facility for drug offenders who pledged to get clean and become productive members of society. Lisa needed transportation to go visit him. I had a car. Because I had nothing to do for the two hours she spent with her boyfriend every weekend, they introduced me to one of his friends, a guy named Marcus.

Marcus had two hobbies, motorcycles and drinking. Like Lisa's boyfriend, he was in the program so he could do less time for the crimes he had committed, crimes he was not allowed to talk about. He had no one else. He needed me. After our first two-hour visit, I was in love.

Between visits, we wrote every day, and spoke on the phone as often as Marcus was allowed. One Saturday I was turned away at the door. During the two hours I waited for Lisa to come out and tell me what happened, I fretted that he no longer loved me. What had I done wrong? How could I get him back? Lisa reported that he had lost his visiting privileges when he sought treatment for an abscessed vein, an ailment that could only come from shooting heroin. As we drove out of the parking lot, he yelled out a window that he loved me. I think he was trying to make sure I wouldn't reject him because of the drugs. No chance of that. I was in love. Clearly, he needed my support more than ever.

Marcus wanted sex. I was one of the few virgins in my high school class. I never really had a boyfriend. I always said that I was saving myself for when I married my true love. But Marcus was my true love, so after much pressure from him, I agreed to lose my virginity.

Marcus planned everything. He figured out the place and organized the lookouts. He led me to an empty room and told me to lay on the floor. It was cold and hard. I was confused, but he assured me that everything was ok, and instructed me to remove one leg of my pants. They were my favorite, green with hounds-tooth print. I had worn them specially for the occasion because he had once complimented me on how good I looked in them.

We only had a few minutes before we would get caught. Still, I guess I expected a little more. I lay on the concrete floor with him on top of me, one leg out of his pants. There was no foreplay, nothing to lead up to pleasure. There was no pleasure. I put my hand across my mouth to keep myself from screaming from the pain.

Suddenly, he jumped to his feet and shoved his leg back into his pants, told me to hurry up and do the same before someone caught us. He didn't expect so much blood, even though he said he had been with other virgins before. He swabbed the bloody floor with his T-shirt and ran back to his room to change before walking me to the door to say good-bye. I was numb. The guard who let me out surely saw the blood soaking the leg of my favorite pants. Lisa and I stopped at a gas station and got paper towels from the bathroom to pack under me so the blood wouldn't ruin the seat of my car.

Mama, who still did my laundry, saw all the blood on my pants and didn't believe me when I said I had unexpectedly started my period early. She called out to Medical Lake, told them about Marcus and what she suspected had happened. He lost visitation privileges for a month. Phone calls and letters weren't enough to sustain his love. He dumped me.

I liked being a nurse's aide. It wasn't my dream job of being a police officer, but I was doing good in the world and leaving it a little better than I found it. I became friends with a co-worker on the evening shift. Dawn was beautiful. She knew how to wear make-up, carry herself, and make people laugh. Everyone liked her. We liked the same music and talked about everything.

Mama hated Dawn. Dawn's mom hated me. They each blamed the other one's daughter for the behaviors of her own. Neither one of us imitated the other. We were just young people looking for fun. It was impossible to simply go home and go to bed after work, so we piled into my car or hers and went driving.

Riverside Drive was the place where young people cruised, driving around and around the same two blocks in downtown Spokane, bumper to bumper, windows down, all tuned to KJRB at full volume, yelling and laughing, and for us, venting after work.

One night, cruising downtown, we caught the attention of a couple of guys in a car, doing the same thing. When we were on opposite sides of the traffic, we leaned out of the car windows and hollered flirtatious comments. Once out of earshot, we raced away and caught back up with each other again. After a few hours of this cat-and-mouse, we met up at Sambos, a 24-hour diner up on Division Street, popular because they had reasonable prices and didn't mind young people being a little loud.

On the way, we plotted our course of action and decided who was going to sit with whom. We handled these guys with our usual flair. Steve, Dawn's choice, said we could order anything, so we ordered steak. His mouth dropped open and we laughed.

We ended up at Dawn's apartment. My guy was named Gordon. I'd not had a sexual encounter since Marcus. This one was just as painful, although Gordon was very nice. It was his first experience. Despite a great deal of effort, our attempt was not successful, though I learned a lot about physiology that night.

After they left, Dawn and I sat up in the wee morning hours re-living our encounters. Dawn wasn't particularly impressed with Steve, but Gordon was so attentive and gentle, we were sure he was The One for me. Except for that name. He needed a name that didn't sound so much like somebody's grandfather. At the same instant we pointed to each other and announced in unison, "Gordie!" That was all I ever called him after that.

All the hoop-la I had heard about sex, however, was false. Sex was what made a man want me. But it was nothing compared to the sensation of being overcome by love with strong arms around me and a promise of protection. This is the kind of love you seek when you have been an unloved child.

Gordie and I drove around a lot, hung out with friends, and played cards with my sister and Daddy.

He was my first experience in a lot of things. Dating. A sexual relationship. Living together. Feeling like an adult.

Like many of the young men from Fairchild Air Force base looking for fun in downtown Spokane, Gordie called himself a flyboy—even though he worked at a desk. On our second date, we drove out to the base so I could see where he lived. On our way there, we passed a dead animal on the side of the road, and I turned my head to look away. He told me how he loved the way I was so sensitive, how he wanted to be the one who protected me from sights like that. We started planning our marriage.

At the base, we drove past the church, the barracks, the commissary, and all through the housing, which looked very modern and grown-up to me, so unlike my garage apartment. All my struggles would melt away if I stepped into a new life as Gordie's wife. He loved music and animals just like I did and had been looking for someone just like me he could take care of. He couldn't imagine himself with a cop for a wife, though. I hardly had time for schoolwork anymore and had pretty much stopped going to classes. My dream of being a police officer slipped away unnoticed.

One evening, several weeks into our romance, we sat side by side in my parents' living room, Mama in her chair, Daddy in his, and Gordie and I on the couch. Gordie told them we had an announcement. We were getting married. I was so nervous that I curled my body against his, hid my face behind his shoulder, and let him do all the talking. Mama had a few questions, such as where we planned to live and how he was going to support me. Gordie answered politely. When Mama asked me if this was what I wanted, I peeked out from behind Gordie's shoulder, giggling like a little kid. "Yes," was the only word I squeaked out in the whole conversation. My parents didn't raise an eyebrow at the fact that we'd hardly known each other for a month, nor did they question my decision to drop out of college.

Mama and I threw ourselves into the wedding preparations. She loved to orchestrate big events and I was happy to do everything she said. We got along better than we ever had. In less than two months, she made me a simple, elegant wedding dress and sent invitations to 500 people. We chose fabric and patterns so each of the bridesmaids could make their dresses. Dawn was to be my Maid of Honor because she was there when Gordie and I met. Mary Tate and Lisa Wilson were also bridesmaids. Gordie and my pastor arranged for the wedding to take place at the church we had seen on my first tour of the base.

When Gordie's parents, brothers, and sister arrived from Nebraska two days before the ceremony, I was very excited to meet my new family, certain that because I was the one their son had chosen, they all would love me. I hit it off with his younger sister Kathy right away, but his mom seemed reserved. She pointedly referred to her son as "Gordon," never using the nickname that even all his friends used now. I would learn later that she did not approve of her son marrying someone from far-away Spokane and probably settling there. We prepared for his family to stay at our apartment, which involved scrubbing everything down and boarding the cats elsewhere because Kathy was allergic. I stayed with Dawn who had a trailer in Airway Heights, the town near the base.

Dawn and Lisa organized one last night of cruising on Riverside. Because we were celebrating a special occasion, we bought some beer. We soon met a couple of fun guys, ditched Dawn's car and took off with them, ending up at their apartment, three of them and three of us. We paired up. I was drunk and only remember flashes. Everyone was in separate rooms. I told the guy, someone whose name I never knew, that I was getting married the next day. He found that extremely funny. I recall being in bed with him. Afterwards, I was ashamed and mortified. I can't call it rape. I didn't say no to getting into their car. I didn't say no when we went to their apartment. When everyone coupled up, I didn't refuse, even though I was doing something I did not want to do. I didn't insist. There were so many times I could have stopped everything. It was over so fast that it was as if nothing had happened. But it had happened.

They drove us back downtown to Dawn's car. Gordie's yellow car was parked next to it. I dove behind the seat. The guys sped past and dropped us off down the block, but Gordie had seen me. Dawn ordered me to walk straight and say nothing. Gordie wasn't going to know anything unless I told him.

Kathy was in Gordie's car with him. Despite our cleaning, she had a bad reaction to the cats and Gordie had been cruising everywhere looking for us so she could stay at Dawn's with me. She went to bed in Dawn's room while Dawn, Lisa, and I sat up the rest of the night talking. I was horrified with myself. The girls both assured me Gordie would never know unless I told him. Kathy heard everything.

I married my first husband through tears of happiness. The weather was perfect. The day was full of music and laughter. My family was pleased. For one beautiful day I was happy.

Gordie surprised me with an expensive night at the Ridpath Hotel. There he did something that was a little strange to me. He already knew about my incontinence and was sympathetic about it. On our wedding night, though, he made me pee the bed for him. I never imagined anyone could find that a turn on. I felt humiliated, but he seemed to be having fun. I pushed the concern aside.

Our honeymoon in Nebraska did not go well. His parents frightened me. His mother was cold. His father lectured me about the duties of a good wife. They warned me not to expect to receive any part of their fortune which, when I looked at my surroundings, seemed non-existent. Gordie's mother told me how she worked nights when Gordie was small, so she tied her four kids to the clothesline during the day so she could sleep. But the kids wailed and cried. The meddlesome neighbors would untie them. Soon she would be awakened, furious, by the sound of them playing in the street. I was unsettled by the visit, but it was easy enough not to remember anything that transpired in Nebraska once we were back in Spokane.

I settled down to life as a new bride with little of the happiness I'd anticipated. Gordie told me he read the Bible and knew God, but I was learning that I hardly knew anything about the man I had married. The only Bible verse he seemed to know was the one about a wife submitting herself to her husband. The wives of flyboys have a special code of conduct, he explained, even though this particular flyboy worked in an office and had never touched an airplane. There would be no singing and no dancing. I could only leave home without him if I was shopping for groceries, and then under a very strict time limit. There was little that I was allowed to do other than serve him.

Sometimes Gordie would shake his head at me and quietly snicker. It was condescending and a little bit frightening.

"What?" I'd ask.

He'd shake his head and snicker a little more.

I spent my time in much the same way I had down in my bedroom at home. When Gordie was at work, I put on music and pretended to be Olivia Newton John, Linda Ronstadt, and Hellen Reddy, always with an eye to the slit in the curtain so I could turn the record player off before Gordie walked in. Even though I sang, "I Am Woman, Hear Me Roar," I couldn't bring myself to stand up to my new husband. My only companions were SnoFee, and the two cats who had triggered Kathy's allergies, Buffy and Benji.

Once we bought a box of Camp Fire Mints. My new husband thought they were made of gold. He set them out on the kitchen counter and forbade me to eat any of them. I love Camp Fire Mints probably more than any other food there is. How could I stay home alone with them all day and not eat even one?

When Gordie counted the Camp Fire Mints that evening and found that two were missing, he was furious. I believe that was when he took the car keys. Or was it the checkbook? Or was I forbidden use of the telephone for the first time? My infractions and his punishments became so frequent I can't keep them straight.

After I married Gordie, things did smooth out with my family. I talked to Mama on the phone every day. She coached me on how to be a good wife, which meant doing everything Gordie wanted and never questioning his authority. We spent many evenings at their house, playing board games and cards. There was a lot of laughing, but it seemed like I was always the butt of one cruel joke or another. Not only was I "dumb," I was "too sensitive."

I have a memory of myself curled like a fetus in a bedroom, sobbing. Mama sat beside me and offered her dubious comfort. I was a married woman now, not a child. You take what your husband dishes up. That's a woman's lot in life. My problem was that I got all riled up when people were just having a little fun.

Many years would go by before I heard the term "gaslighting."

One evening, about six months after the wedding, Dawn stopped by without warning. It was a typical evening. Gordie was in the bedroom watching a basketball game. I was supposed to stay within earshot in case he needed a sandwich. Lights would waste too much expensive electricity, so I wasn't allowed to have them on. I sat on the floor in my usual corner, the record player next to me softly playing "Goodbye Yellow Brick Road." Gordie didn't hear me let her in. She was appalled.

I kept shushing her, but she finally convinced me to sneak out to her car. I told her everything. She told me I couldn't go back in there. She had moved in with her parents, so I couldn't go home with her, but she pledged to help me all the same. We called my parents from a phone booth. Mama told me to get myself back home fast. A husband treats his wife however he wants. If it was a mistake to marry him, it was my mistake to live with. No use crying now. Dawn grabbed the phone receiver. She told Mama she didn't understand and described how she had found me. Mama, who didn't like Dawn anyway, ordered her to take me back to Gordie and mind her own business.

We set off to cruise Riverside and figure out what to do next. Dawn spotted a high school friend walking along the side of the road. Daniel. She swung her car around and picked him up. He knew of a place we could stay. Dawn dropped us off and we spent the night there in an attic bedroom. Although I did not want to, we had sex on a mattress on the floor.

The next day Dawn took us to an abandoned house she knew on the southeast side of town. A few runaways were squatting there. The house had electricity so there was heat from the open oven door. By the second day I had fallen in love with Daniel. It felt like such a lark. I could laugh and be myself. The runaways liked me. I enjoyed doing without, relying on a few teenage boys to steal food, and shivering most of the time. We spent most of our days playing a board game in the dining room. Dawn came to visit often. The boys loved her, too. I had a family. My troubles were over.

Then I got sick, very sick, with a relentless cough and a high fever. Daniel and the boys were scared and didn't want me there anymore. I had to get to a warm place with decent food. Mama still wouldn't take me in, so Dawn drove me back to my husband. He laid out his conditions. Dawn was never to return. I was to relinquish my checkbook and the keys to the car and house. Gordie would take the telephone to work with him. I was to stay inside and keep the curtains closed. The record player was off limits. So was the television.

I was too sick to refuse.

Over the course of the next month, as I recovered, I realized I was pregnant. Gordie wanted to know if the baby was his. Despite his having had three sisters, he knew nothing about the workings of women. In the second week of our marriage, I had to explain to him what a period was. I should have just told him the baby was his, but I told him the truth. It might be his. Or it might be Daniel's.

"We will treat it as if it were mine," he pronounced. We were never to speak of it again.

I was allowed to make friends with Lucy, another Air Force wife who lived up the hill from us. She was pregnant as well. Gordie deemed her trustworthy. He returned the car keys and checkbook so we could shop together for our babies. We spent happy after-noons scouring thrift stores for cribs, strollers, and baby clothes. Then Gordie decided he didn't like living on the base, so he moved us to a little house in Spokane. My friendship with Lucy faded.

Gordie's parents moved in with us to help. His mother was the expert. I was incompetent, which I demonstrated by having heartburn when I ate her greasy cooking. Any complaints or requests for more bland food demonstrated how ungrateful I was.

Despite all my discomfort and unhappiness, Jeremy came easily into the world, tiny and perfect, two weeks before his due date. I had no anesthesia and nursed him right away. I stared at him constantly, watched him change and grow daily. I wanted to memorize everything about him. Gordie's parents returned to Nebraska. I settled in and nursed, cuddled, and played with my baby. For the most part Gordie ignored us, but this was not as painful as it had been. I had Jeremy. The love that flowed between us was the same as God's love which surrounded us. That was all I cared about.

When Jeremy was a little over a year old, I discovered I was pregnant again. This pregnancy was filled with stress and difficulty caused by Gordie's endless restrictions and mental abuse. I began cramping and spotting, so the doctor ordered bedrest after my fifth month. Gordie objected—to me, not the doctor. He refused to do without anything a wife was supposed to supply—food on demand, an immaculate house, uniforms ironed just-so, a perfectly-behaved one-year-old, sex.

He moved us back on the base where doctors, shopping, and my friend Lucy were nearby. He wouldn't have to alter his routine to help me. Lucy called every day and visited often with her little girl who was Jeremy's age. She shopped for me and helped me keep my house organized. But there was no way all the stress could be removed from my home.

Shortly before Jeremy's second birthday, eight weeks before the baby was due, the contractions would not stop. I was admitted into the hospital and within a day, my premature baby girl arrived. For someone so tiny, the delivery was an ordeal. The doctors gave me a spinal that was supposed to make it all easier. I screamed in pain when the needle was inserted into my spine, then, even worse, came the numbness. I watched them lift me onto the delivery table as if they were moving a scarecrow, worried about what the drugs were doing to my baby. I couldn't push, so the doctor placed his hands on my abdomen and leaned down so hard his feet left the floor.

Because the birth was such a strain, the nurses convinced me to take a little morphine to help with the pain. I was instantly sorry. A green version of the Stay-Puft Marshmallow man set himself up to oversee everything from a corner of the room. I called the nurses in to see, and of course, they saw no one. I giggled along with the nurses and hid how upset I was. I vowed never to take morphine again.

All this difficulty was offset by the fact that my baby was beautiful, perfect. Her little lungs were not fully formed, so they placed her on life support in the nursery. To see her, I often had to push past an admiring crowd in front of the nursery window. She couldn't nurse yet, but I wanted her to have the colostrum, so I used a breast pump from the very start and they tube-fed it to my baby. Apparently, I got a little gung-ho, because soon I was pumping enough milk for all the other babies in the NICU. Years later, we discovered ourselves living next door to a pair of twins who had received my milk.

Two weeks later, when we were allowed to take her home, my daughter weighed four pounds. Her little head fit perfectly into the palm of my hand. Only doll clothes were small enough to fit her. She was so pretty, and so sensitive. No matter how soft I made the surface of the changing table and how gently I laid her down, she screamed out in pain when her skin touched any surface that was not my skin.

I cooked, vacuumed, and played with Jeremy, all with this tiny child cradled on my forearm and held close under my shirt. She nursed whenever she needed to. Once we embarrassed both myself and a delivery man when I had to switch arms so I could sign for a package.

Gordie kept forgetting her name.

The Pill gave me debilitating headaches, but my cycles were very regular, so we used what is called the rhythm method for contraception. Gordie didn't want to hear any details about it. I kept a calendar and would warn Gordie when we had entered the dangerous days of the month. This worked. Or it could have.

Gordie was convinced sex was his right. He used Bible-talk to proclaim that as his wife, it was my duty to keep him satisfied. Often, he would wake me in the night for sex. When I would caution that we were in the week when I could get pregnant, he would say, "We'll just love it like the others." That actually sounded pretty nice to me. My love for my two babies was at the center of my happiness. Another baby would bring even more love into our lives.

By this time, Gordie was out of the Air Force and taking any kind of job he could find. For a while he was selling something door to door in Montana. We spoke on the phone daily. When I discovered I was pregnant, I was excited and told him right away. He was upset.

Because he was out of town at the time I found out I was pregnant, Gordie decided the baby wasn't his. Hard as I tried, I could not convince him otherwise. He refused to absorb any explanations about how conception occurred well before you were certain you were pregnant. Not even the doctor could get him to understand. As far as he was concerned, this pregnancy didn't have anything to do with him, so he would not be tolerating any disruption because of it.

At five months I started to have contractions. Because my last baby had come so early, they put me in the hospital, leaving Gordie at home in charge of a high-spirited preschooler and a toddler. When he visited me, he would berate me, hissing angrily that I was "putting him through this," ordering me to quit all this faking and get back home. The hospital staff noticed how the contractions would start up every time he visited. They listened at the door. There were strong warnings. Soon Gordie was banned.

The doctors were concerned about a precipitous delivery, one where the baby comes suddenly and extremely fast. They positioned an incubator outside the hospital room in case there wasn't time to get to the delivery room.

I missed my children so much, but the staff kept my spirits up. Week after week we celebrated every day that I was still pregnant. Finally, six weeks early, I gave birth to a beautiful baby girl. Gordie was there, happy it was over so I could get back to my neglected housework. Soon I was introducing their new little sister to my two small children, all of us hugging and so happy.

I settled into a pleasant life with my three little ones. Their existence was what I focused on, and being a good mother was all I strived for. With all of Gordie's restrictions, I had a lot of time to play with them. They were funny and creative. I loved looking into their sweet, honest faces as they explained something to me. All the ways that Gordie was difficult were just obstacles I had to tolerate. Mama supported me in this. Not until many years later would I hear the term "emotional abuse" used to describe what Mama called "a woman's lot in life."

Gordie became more and more controlling. He came home one day and found me playing with the children in the yard. For a mother of three, I looked "too good," he said. His father had been right. You marry an attractive woman and you're going to spend your whole life worried about other men. Hadn't I already proved it? I was far too attractive to be out in the front yard where other men could see me, Gordie decided. I was no longer allowed to leave the house, not even step onto the porch, while he was at work.

Gordie was so obsessed with money that even a family picnic in the park was something we couldn't afford. He saw buying a home, not as an investment, but as going into debt. Despite his resistance, we did manage to buy a house. I handled the bills, but he complained that hard as he worked, he never had enough spending money in his wallet. I gave in and let him handle the budget, and within a couple of months we were so far behind that we almost lost our electricity.

Our home felt like a jail. The closest thing I got to support was Mama's daily encouragement to accept my lot and obey my husband. It was summer. The heat was stifling. Indoors, day after day, I exhausted my creativity trying to keep the children from being restless. I started sneaking with them to Minnehaha Park, three blocks away. They played while I sat beneath a tree, reading the Bible, anxiously glancing up every few minutes, afraid that my husband would come home early for some reason and catch me there.

Difficult as they were, I loved those times, hour after hour in the park, all summer long. The children were so happy. I was able to read the Bible from cover to cover. I became more enlightened regarding the man's role in a marriage. He was supposed to honor the work his wife did and treat her with love and care. I started resenting my husband.

Eventually Gordie allowed me to leave the house alone—to go back to work. I found a job in a care center at a retirement home. I worked the night shift so there would be no need for daycare. It could have worked. When I got back from my shift at the retirement center, I took over childcare responsibilities and Gordie went to work. When he got home, I went to sleep. Unfortunately, the man I married was incapable of handling the smallest crisis regarding children, and his evenings were full of crises. If I got four hours of uninterrupted sleep, I considered it a good rest.

Exhausted, I went to the doctor and found out I was pregnant again. Delighted at the prospect of another little one, and relieved that there was a reason for my extreme fatigue, I rode the bus to where Gordie was working in a grocery store way up on North Division Street. On the bus ride, I grew anxious about telling my husband that I was six weeks pregnant.

When I sought him out in the back room of the grocery store, his response was even worse than I had feared. With little care for the customers or other workers present in the store, he went into a rage, picking up can after can of vegetables and hurling them at me, yelling that I was a whore and a slut, shouting "How could you do this!" as if it was my fault alone that I was pregnant. Nobody intervened. I took the stoning. Finally, he marched me out of the store, bloodied and sobbing. As we passed the cashier, she wagged her head in disgust.

His ranting continued as we drove to the daycare to retrieve the children. He carried on the whole time I fixed dinner and put them to bed.

I was on my way into the shower when I saw the blood running down my legs. I laid on the couch, on the phone with my doctor, explaining that yes, the bleeding was much more than with a period. I was listening to him organize a trip to the emergency room when Gordie yanked the phone out of the wall. Realizing he'd be called out if he did nothing, he piled the children into the cab of the pickup, threw a mattress in the back, and ordered me to ride there. The cramping was terrible. I moaned in agony while Gordie, feigning concern, delivered the children to a friend's house.

At the hospital, my doctor was as worried about my emotional state as my physical one. Gordie called my pastor who rushed to the hospital and comforted him while I received a very painful D&C without anesthesia. I cried, more for the death of my child than the pain of the procedure.

When we got home, Gordie announced that he was exhausted and had to be at work in a couple of hours. I was left to bring the sleeping children in from the truck. Last thing before he went to bed, he ordered me to clean up the mess I had left on our beautiful white couch lest the stains set before morning.

My physical and emotional pain were transformed into a greater rage that I had ever experienced. I just wanted him out of my life.

I don't remember which one of us flung which cruel remark first, or all the insults we traded up until the moment he was packing his things and leaving. I do remember the tug-of-war we had over my purse. I had just cashed my check and he succeeded in driving away in our only operating vehicle with every last dime I had. The memory of that night that pains me most of all was going up to the children's room after it was quiet and finding six-year-old Jeremy at the bedroom window, tears streaming down his face. His father had just packed his things and driven away. I couldn't comfort him because I was so glad Gordie was gone.

My parents took Gordie in.

Over the course of the next year, Gordie and I hammered out the ever-changing details of our divorce daily, with much shouting, phone-slamming, and me accosting the children with the latest outrage committed by their father. I wanted them to hate Gordie and love me. That's how I would punish him. For making me a prisoner in my own home. For the death of my baby. For failing to fill the black hole in my heart with love.

I never told the children that I wanted to hear how they were doing, nor did I ask what they felt. If they ever mentioned their father, I twisted what they said into a story about how terrible he was. I told Jeremy that Gordie wasn't his biological dad. I don't remember if anyone told us to stop. If they did, it fell on deaf ears.

It feels like the most natural thing in the world to do this. When the children visited Gordie or my parents, they heard hateful accusations about me. None of us could stop. If I could change the past, I would allow myself to recognize that I was filled with rage, fear, and pain. I would acknowledge that the marriage was over and find help in healing myself and my children so we could move on. Then all that happened from this point on would have been different. There's no way to do that. But I cannot wish any harder that there was.

I believed that the children came from my body and were mine. If the father left his family, he forfeited his right to them. That was fine with Gordie. He didn't want the trouble and expense of having the children around. He didn't ask for visitation. I was glad.

I jump-started my old dreams and got a job in a detective agency. I found a three-bedroom house close to my work, managed to furnish it and buy some toys for the children. I was good at my job. Since I was the only female there, they gave me the cases no one else wanted, most of them having to do with children, iron-ically—child custody and tracking down long-lost parents. One case was of a son searching for the father he'd never known. When I got the two of them together, they sent me a dozen long stemmed roses. In another case, I was hired by a mother concerned about the safety of her son who lived with his dad on the reservation in Wellpinit. The dad was believed to be dealing drugs. That case was very dangerous, considering we were three white people under cover at a Native American Powwow.

The PI work didn't pay enough to support me, the three small children, and the necessary daycare required for me to go to work. So I went on Public Assistance, which meant that the state came after Gordie for child support. It didn't take Gordie long to figure out that if he had custody, he wouldn't have to pay.

The children spent a weekend with Mama and did not return at the time we'd agreed upon. She had helped Gordie go to court and get temporary custody. He evicted the renters from the house we owned, and moved in. His parents came up from Nebraska to tend the children so he would not have to pay daycare. I had to fight to get visitation. Nothing they had done was legal. Eventually I regained custody.

For the children, it was months of never being certain which parent was going to snatch them away from the other one forever. The girls were very young, not able to follow all the ins and outs of our hatred for each other. But Jeremy, who loved us both and heard it all, was six, and then seven. He was so very clever, but not clever enough to process all that venom.

After I regained custody, Gordie was stingy about any of the children's needs. When one of them (probably Jeremy) wanted something, I would tell him his dad was supposed to buy it. Gordie, of course, said that he paid child support so that I could buy it. Or he would make promises that he didn't keep. The upshot was that Jeremy never got what he asked for.

Once, it was a pool table. Jeremy asked for one for Christmas, and his dad agreed that it was a fine idea. They talked about all the fun they would have with it. Jeremy believed him and told all his friends. I warned him that his dad would not come through. I warned Gordie about leading him on. Gordie countered that no kid would be serious about getting a pool table for Christmas. But Jeremy believed him. On Christmas he was crushed. His friends laughed.

His mother said, "I told you so." As if that would make him feel loved and secure.

I wanted my children to know they were beautiful and valuable. I tried to make their lives as happy as I could. The message I tried to convey was that we were a team, a family who worked together for the same goals. I tried to be honest with them and always keep my promises. Before a trip to the grocery store, I listed everything we were going to buy and reminded them about what we were definitely not going to buy.

We would set out for the store in our pickup truck, windows down, singing along with the radio as it blasted Aretha Franklin and Olivia Newton John. At traffic lights, the people pointed and laughed with us. Jeremy started to find that embarrassing.

In the grocery store, they set forth on "missions" to get the various items on our list. When the shopping was successfully finished, we often had a picnic in Riverfront Park. They understood that we couldn't spend money, but the park had many places for us to explore. There were slides, jungle gyms, and a sandbox. They loved tossing sticks off the bridge over the river and watching the current catch them and sweep them off towards Spokane Falls.

I vowed not to discipline them the way Daddy had disciplined us. My children were precious and vulnerable. I refused to subject them to the humiliation that I experienced. Severe misbehavior that continued past a third warning merited a "whoopin'" which amounted to three swats on the behind—only three and fully clothed, enough to sting a little, and never the kind of beating that could bruise their buttocks and thighs. Nobody ever got knocked into a wall or the furniture by an unexpected slap across the face. I didn't turn my children into an outlet for my rage. Well, except when I poisoned them with all my angry opinions about their father.

I was very strict about what they could watch on television. No violence. Not even Bugs Bunny or Road Runner. I didn't like the message these shows sent where the good guy recovers instantly from the gunshot or bomb blast and the bad guy never gets punished. I wanted them to learn kindness and honesty. In the evenings, we watched shows that I selected. When they fell asleep, I carried them to their beds.

I should have been satisfied with the life that we had together. But I had mental health issues that went far beyond Gordie's emotional abuse. The scars of my childhood lay in wait for me, poised for ambush. I told myself I was a good mom. I was certainly the best mom I knew how to be.

I wish I could have lived in person what I tried to teach them.

Once the divorce was final, it was time to find someone to replace Gordie and be a proper male role model for the children, especially Jeremy. Without anything in my experience to demonstrate what such a partnership might look like, I had no idea how to find it. The best place to look seemed to be where the men were, so I started looking in bars.

I wasn't much of a drinker. My parents both grew up in families that suffered the ravages of alcohol. It was banished from our house. There was never a discussion about alcohol's allure and consequences. The few times that I had over-sampled alcohol, I never connected it to the way it made me feel and the bad decisions I made.

In my PI work, I became comfortable in a bar called Lucky's. Lucky, the proprietor, had gone to high school with Mama and, I think, thought he could use me to get friendly with her again. He knew I was undercover but didn't let on. He protected me. When I walked in, he called out, "There's my daughter!" and poured me a drink on the house. By the time that drink was finished, someone else would have bought me another.

Lucky, and nearly everyone who patronized his bar, was Black. In this new circle of friends I was certain not to run into aunts, uncles, cousins, or any of Gordie's friends. I met some very inappropriate individuals, although those individuals could probably say the same thing about me. I left my children at home with a list of instructions and phone numbers to call (never my parents or Gordie!) if they had a problem. Sometimes they contacted me with minor issues while I was out. They said they were fine. I believed them and repeated this lie to myself over and over. You can do this when you have a black hole in your heart.

3. A Man Who Will Protect Me

I met Phil Taylor at the Riverside Bar, a dingier, scarier place up the block from Lucky's. Prostitutes, drug dealers, and their customers hung out, played pool, and did business. There were nightly fights and stabbings out back. Not the kind of place for a young mother of three to find a stable partner and role model for her children, but there I was.

I was drinking, minding my own business, when a girl came in and started yelling at me, calling me a Snitch Bitch. If I didn't already know what she was mad about, I would have been scared that information about my PI days was about to be made public. Even if that didn't happen, I had a reputation to protect. I was white and a regular in a Black bar. I didn't want anyone calling me a snitch for any reason.

When the woman accosted me, I jumped up and asked who the hell was calling me a snitch. I wasn't much of a fighter, really didn't know how, but I raised my arm in front of her face to give it a try. Before any blows could land, a pair of iron-strong arms grabbed me from behind, hoisted me up, and carried me, literally kicking and screaming, out of the bar. When he let go of me, I turned to see someone I didn't know. He told me that he had noticed me many times (a white woman in a bar full of Black people, how astute an observer!) He had often thought it would be great to meet me. (How many times have I fallen for that one?) He had just rescued me from certain peril, so of course I was immediately attracted to him. We walked to another bar down the street, and I filled in all the details of what had just happened.

Weeks prior, Lisa Wilson, my former bridesmaid, the friend who had introduced me to Marcus, convinced me to loan my car to her brother so he could go to the welfare office and run a few other errands. She didn't mention his plan to use it in a bank robbery which was caught on camera. I got the car back and did notice that the police seemed to be shadowing me, but I had no clue why. Eventually a detective confronted me and asked a million questions about a bank robbery I knew nothing about. I told him about loaning the car to Lisa's brother. That led to his arrest. His wife was the woman who wanted to beat me up.

After I explained all this to Phil, we returned to the Riverside. By the time we got there, we were in love. Or at least I was. People were all over me asking questions, and Phil, my hero, vouched that I was no snitch. We were inseparable from that moment on.

Becoming inseparable first involved bringing Phil home and kicking out the drifter who was already staying there, someone I obviously didn't care about all that much. Phil and the drifter got into a fight (over me!) I fled. Some neighbors saw me running, thought they were both after me, and called the police who settled the affair. I realize now that if either of them had another place to sleep that night, they wouldn't have fought for a place in my bed.

Less than a month after we got together, when the children were spending a week with their father, Phil went out in the evening and didn't come home for two days. I was anxious and worried the whole time he was gone, angry, too. All those feelings disappeared when he returned because I was so happy to have him back. Apparently, we were going to discuss what occurred later, because he went straight to bed.

Then there was a tap on the door. It was a man I didn't know, asking to talk to Phil. I kind of wanted to talk to Phil myself. I let his friend in and woke him up. While Phil got himself together, I made polite small talk to his friend. Then the guy changed his mind and left before Phil came out.

I was snatched before I registered anything. At first he slapped me, then he started punching me with his fists as if I were a grown man. I ran into the bedroom, tripped, and fell. As he kicked me under the bed, I wondered how I was going to fit. I heard his friend's car start and drive off. Had he been listening the whole time and done nothing?

Phil dragged me out by the arm, stood me up and punched me, hard. I fell on the bed and lay there. He walked out.

Why, I wondered. Why? It was the only word my brain could form. I had never been punched like that before. What had I done wrong? I felt so much shame by the time Phil came back, I actually apologized. He told me not to ever let a man into his house again and I promised I wouldn't. I had meant no disrespect.

Later, as we lay in bed together, I told him I was a bit angry and that he should never hit me again. He said I could hit him if it would make me feel better. I think he was bluffing because he seemed surprised when I sat up and gave him an elbow in his face, as hard as I could, not once, but multiple times before he stopped me. That felt real good. Problem solved.

Both Phil and I were born in August, so I romantically bought him a pickup truck the lime-green color of our birthstones. He promptly disappeared in the truck and was gone for three days. When he arrived home, he told me where the truck had broken down and went straight to bed.

I set out on foot to find the truck, which I would later discover just happened to be parked across from his ex-girlfriend's house. Soon I realized it was too far to walk there. At that point I was six months pregnant with the baby I hoped was Phil's and not the drifter's, the guy he had kicked out that first night we were together.

I was familiar with East Sprague Avenue, the "ho stroll" that bustled with activity all hours of the day and night. I figured that a pregnant lady could find a ride there to go get her truck and bring it home. Sure enough, after a few blocks, a green Jeep pulled up next to me. I explained that I wasn't a prostitute, just someone who was looking for a ride to her vehicle. The driver seemed very nice and agreed to help me. When we arrived, the truck refused to start.

He offered to take me to his place to fetch a tow rope so I could get my truck back home. Instead, he drove up onto Beacon Hill, a short-cut to his house, he said. It was located in an obscure spot on the other side. I must have been born yesterday because I went along without protest.

He stopped on top of Beacon Hill, got out, walked around to my side, and opened the door with a crowbar in his hand. He grabbed me and threw me down, stomach-first, with great deal of force, finishing with a smack across my back with the crowbar. I thought of my baby, that it was probably already gone, and gave its fate to God. He held the crowbar over my head and ordered me to undress. I rolled over, put up my hand to block another hit and started to talk. I assured him as calmly as I could that he could do whatever he pleased and I would not fight him.

He seemed disappointed but did not use any further force. I struggled not show any of the terror going on inside me. I focused my mind on God's love and prayed that I would get out of this alive.

He finished his repulsive business on my stomach, disgusted, I think, with how easy it had been. I felt a little victorious to have deprived him of that thrill. He told me not to move, retrieved my purse from the vehicle, threw it into the weeds, and drove off. I got dressed, except for my pantyhose, which I left to mark the spot where I was raped.

I got myself to a 7-11 and called the police. Contractions were beginning. I was crying, dirty, hurting and could barely keep my head. I felt more shame at not having done enough to protect my baby than I did over what had just happened to me. They connected me with Rape Crisis and sent an ambulance.

At the hospital, the contractions slowed down and the baby's heartbeat was strong. They were kind and assured me I had done the right thing. If I had fought to protect my baby, we both could have been killed. They ran a light over my abdomen where the rapist had deposited his business. They took samples and pictures. The doctor came in and told me he believed I was telling the truth and would be a witness.

Detectives arrived. They were pretty sure they knew who my rapist was but could only bring him to justice if I was willing to testify. If I didn't, he might do something worse to his next victim.

Phil burst in, pushed past the detectives, and scooped me up in his arms.

"They wouldn't give me any details, just that you had been hurt. Oh Baby, I was so scared."

Apparently if a woman says she was raped and the man who rushes to her side is Black, she's a prostitute and it wasn't rape after all. The detectives said they'd be in touch and left. I was never able to reach them. Later I was told that the evidence had gotten lost somehow.

A couple of mornings later, I woke up to the dogs barking ferociously and someone pounding on the door. It was the police. They were looking for someone named William Taylor. I answered truthfully that I knew no one named William. They showed me a picture of a clean-shaven black man. Phil had a beard, so I truthfully told them I knew of no one that looked like that. They said they had the house surrounded. I responded that my children were sleeping inside. They asked who else was in the house. I told them I did not have to tell them that. They said they were prepared to enter the house with force.

At that point, Phil called to me and said to tell them he would go peacefully. I argued with him. I knew from my law enforcement training that they couldn't enter the house without probable cause, but Phil said that was only true if you were white. He was concerned for the kids. I respected him for that. When I let the cops in, they threw him against the wall and undertook a thorough and humiliating search of his person. The warrant was for several consolidated charges, none of them violent, none of them felonies, things like drug possession and driving with expired tags. He offered no resistance and still they treated him like a murderer. It took me over a week to get him out of jail.

Two nights after his arrest, someone knocked at the door and the dogs went off again. The kids were asleep. With the chain still on, I asked who it was.

"You remember. We had such a good time up on Beacon Hill the other day," he responded. "Just thought I'd stop by and see how you were doing here all by yourself."

"How did you know where I live?" I demanded.

"Oh, we have mutual friends," he answered.

I let the dogs out the back door. They circled the house as they were trained to do. I heard a man scream. The dogs came to the front door. No one was there when I let them in.

Phil was certain the baby wasn't his. He had one child when he was very young. In all the intervening years, he never used protection and never had another. I argued that he couldn't know whether the women he'd been with had used birth control or had abortions. Maybe he had dozens of children from one-night stands that he never knew about. Everyone at our local watering hole got in on the debate. Phil's friends were equally certain the baby couldn't be his.

I did not want to believe these things. I wanted my baby to be Phil's and so I was going to believe that it was his. The only relationship scenario in my head was fall-in-love-have-a-baby. I couldn't envision anything else. I didn't want the baby to be the drifter's. I liked him well enough, but never loved him. He was nice, which I found boring and weak. I wanted a bad boy like Phil to be my love.

During the pregnancy, I dreamed of being handed a blonde, blue-eyed baby. I would scream in the dream and run up and down the halls of the hospital shouting they'd given me the wrong baby and demanding my real one. In my waking life, I was confident that the baby I carried was Black.

Worried about another miscarriage, I limited my activities and usually stayed home while Phil went out. He loved his pot, cocaine, alcohol and, as it turned out, women. I would lie awake at home, listening for a car, voices, or any sound that told me he was home. Night after night. Trapped again. I blamed Phil, definitely not the baby. I loved the baby, and I knew the baby would love me.

Daytime wasn't so bad. I had girlfriends. Other women like me, in love with bad boys. We got together at each other's houses, played records, laughed, and complained about our men. My friend Alice was going to be my delivery coach, but she didn't have a car. Phil needed the pickup for whatever it was he did all day. We were all worried about a sudden, premature labor. Alice put the taxi companies on alert. If they got a call from me, they were to pick her up on the way to my house. That was the fastest route to get us both to the hospital. We had a few dry runs because my labor kept starting and stopping. Alice and the taxi drivers would be somber and concerned on the way to the hospital. Then we all celebrated when I went home with the baby still inside me. They felt like my family.

No one in my blood family knew I was pregnant.

Phil spent more and more time out drinking and who knows what else. When he did come home, he was difficult to deal with. He came home one night in a blackout. We got into an argument. He shoved me, hard, onto the bed. I bounced back up and reminded him about the baby. He was able to stop himself and left. In the morning he was back. One moment the children and I were asleep and the next thing we knew, the door was laying on the kitchen floor and Phil was standing in the wide-open doorway.

The baby came six weeks early. The cab plan worked fine and my baby boy was born in song and love and laughter. He was healthy and beautiful, blonde and blue-eyed, with balls black as coal. Phil showed up a couple of hours later, picked him up and carried him to the window.

"You named this white-ass baby after me?"

It started with a birthday party, I think, something that had to do with one of the children. Friends were coming for dinner and bringing their families. There was to be cake and presents. Phil volunteered to run out and get some ice cream.

We waited and waited and finally started the party without him. I was embarrassed. The children were distressed when I put them to bed and Phil still wasn't home. The friends said not to worry. I wasn't worried. I was pissed.

Another time when Phil had stayed out all night, he was furious when he came home in the morning to find that there was no hot food for him to eat. This time I kept the food warm on the stove, stirring it so it wouldn't burn. I paced up and down to stay awake. All night long. And into the next day.

When he came home, he dished up his dinner and took it outside to eat at the backyard table. It was a beautiful summer morning. I stood there watching him in silence. He didn't look up.

"We need to talk," I said.

"About what?"

He couldn't have said anything worse than that. An explosion went off inside me. I upended the table, spilling overcooked greens, black-eyed peas, and ham hocks all over him.

Slowly, he set the table straight, set his plate back where it was, and scooped his food off his lap and back onto the plate. He resumed eating. I was holding a can of root beer, which I pitched at his head, hard. It bounced off his forehead and spun around like a pinwheel, spraying its contents. I walked backwards towards the house yelling about how I deserved an explanation and an apology. He picked up his plate and followed me in but turned to go upstairs. I jumped in his way.

I couldn't hear the kids, but I figured they were upstairs in their rooms. He tried to shove me out of the way. There was an open window at the foot of the stairs, so I leaned back against the steps to brace myself and shoved him out the window with my foot. He landed on the ground with his feet still on the windowsill.

Everything was in slow motion by then. Next thing, a pair of black hands were planted on the frame of the window, fingers splayed. As he pulled himself through, I remember saying, "Oh shit!" and racing into the bathroom. Don't run into the bathroom. You'll be trapped.

Phil shoved the bathroom door in and punched me square in the nose. Bones broke with a crunch. Blood sprayed into the bathtub, on the floor, the walls, even the ceiling. (Who do you think cleaned it up?)

Then the worst part happened. My parents came to the door.

I grabbed a towel to sop the blood that still flowed freely from my broken nose and sat on the couch. I placed a finger on each side of the broken bone, trying to straighten it, holding it tight. Phil sat with his head in his hands. Later, he said he thought he was going to go to jail. That's not what happened.

I don't know what I expected them to do. Get mad? Defend me? Offer help? Lecture about domestic violence?

Mama sat down next to Phil and gave him a little fake punch on the shoulder, "Now let's not do that again," she teased.

Daddy shook his head at me and said, "You know, sometimes you can really be hard to live with."

I bolted from my chair and out the back door, running through the yard, out the gate, across the alley, and into a field where I heard footsteps pounding behind me. Then I was slammed, tackled from behind. I spat out dirt and weeds while Phil whispered in my ear, "I'm sorry. I'm so sorry. They are terrible. I had no idea."

He didn't exactly apologize for hitting me. Maybe it was justified, like my parents said. I was *bad,* after all. I had to do better.

Phil found work in Reno and we moved. We had more fights. I became adept at aligning the bones in my re-broken nose. Eventually I found myself, four kids, a dog, a turtle, and whatever other possessions would fit in a pickup on the way to a shelter in Sacramento. We had directions on a slip of paper and got lost in the web of highways, the kids yelling out their "help." We actually had fun.

In no time, I was sharing an apartment in Broderick, a suburb of Sacramento, with another single mother. The apartment complex we moved into was huge, with a swimming pool, and a center courtyard full of swings and other toys for the kids to play on. Our apartment had two bedrooms and an air conditioner. It was stiflingly hot. 105 degrees was not uncommon. The only time it was safe for the kids to play outside was in the middle of the night when it was a little cooler. So we all switched our days and nights, sleeping inside with the air conditioner on during the day and everyone going outside during the nighttime hours. The kids played out in the courtyard while the mothers watched them from their balconies, radios on full volume, all playing the same station. Like me, most of them came from other places, here to make a new start.

It didn't take long—maybe a week—before my life felt empty and off-course without a man. I became a regular at the bar on the highway just outside the complex. I started dating a junkie who was cute and funny until, during an argument, he scratched me on the chest hard enough to draw blood. I took a swing at him with a cast iron frying pan. He yelled for help. Suddenly the manager was at the door. She talked me down. The junkie ran out the door. The manager and I were suddenly laughing.

Later I realized my truck was missing.

I tracked down some of his friends who told me where the truck had been dumped. The canopy over the bed was gone, but it still ran. Without the canopy, we mothers would load all the kids in back and go shopping, to the laundromat, and the food giveaway. Once we even took a trip to the zoo. Sometimes a couple of us moms left the kids behind and went cruising by ourselves, which is how I spotted Derek talking to some friends in a front yard and hit the brakes.

He could have stepped off the pages of a magazine he was so beautiful. My friend egged me on. He returned my smile and sauntered over, checking me out as we talked. The next thing I knew, we were on a date. Then we were living together. Later, he told me that if I hadn't slept with him that first night he wouldn't have been interested. Of course I slept with him. I was already head-over-hells in love.

At some point, Derek confessed to me that he liked cocaine. I had always stayed away from drugs, even though Phil had done them. Derek urged me to try, but I refused. Cocaine, it turned out, was an everyday thing for him. He had lots of friends who gave it to him. I could tell he enjoyed it. He started getting high in front of me when we went out, and at home, with the children sleeping in the next room.

One night we were relaxing together, drinking and laughing. The kids were asleep in the next room. I caught the giggles and fell back on the bed, head swirling, enjoying being drunk with Derek beside me, running his hands up and down my arm, telling me how much he loved me.

I didn't notice him getting the needle ready, didn't notice him finding the vein, barely even felt the prick. Then I wasn't drunk anymore, I was floating in an ecstasy I had never known. It was the very best thing that had ever happened to me. Yes, some people do get hooked on the first hit.

Addiction is a disease of the mind and body. This is a hard idea for many to wrap their minds around. Addicts are cast as people who are the cause of their own problems, victims of their own weakness. People point out that addicts don't get *infected* with their condition. Nor do they get cured by medication. Many people think that by calling addiction a disease addicts duck responsibility for what they are doing to themselves.

We must think harder about what diseases are. Consider the way that exposure to environmental toxins can unlock a cancer cell or cause an immune system to go awry. Diseases like melanoma, fibromyalgia, or multiple sclerosis aren't caused by infections or reliably cured by treatments like medication or surgery. With diseases like these, the body attacks itself.

Illnesses of the mind aren't caused by germs. There is no pill that reliably cures depression or schizophrenia. People don't suffer from these conditions because they are weak. Some of them, PTSD for instance, are known to be caused by exposure to toxic emotional situations.

Because addiction is a disease of the mind and body, these two parts of you work together to keep you sick. The body tells the mind that you will die unless you get the sweet relief the addiction offers. The afflicted mind believes the body and focuses solely on how to find more of what the body is craving.

I believe that the root cause of my cocaine addiction is what people now call "relationship addiction." Falling in love affects me as powerfully as what comes out of a needle shoved into a vein. Rationality goes out the window. Consequences disappear. I also believe that the root cause of my relationship addiction was the abuse and neglect I endured as a child.

Without tools for understanding my experience, I did not develop a healthy balance of the hormones and brain chemicals that rule a person's moods and decision-making. Instead, I have a black hole in the place where love and connection belong. No romantic relationship can fill it. You could say that my disease is my desperation to do the impossible and fill it anyway. All sorts of inappropriate people with their own issues see me coming from miles away. We "click."

A relationship addiction easily leads to the kinds of relationships where you will get the exposure that brings about a drug addiction, too.

It's taken me more than a half-century to figure that out.

Addicted I was. I had to have it. At first, I could only have it at the beginning of the month when I got my check. It didn't take long before a month was too long to wait. Soon the child support money that came in the middle of the month started going to the dope man. Even then, I was only getting high two nights a month, when the kids were asleep. I couldn't say no to this new friend. We started going to a motel, leaving the three children for days, asking neighbors to "keep an eye on them." It was the best and worst time of my life.

Derek's daughter appeared one day. Her mother dropped her off saying she "needed a break." Tamara was smart and beautiful. She was five, the same age as my daughter. They got along so well that people thought they were sisters, even though one was Black and one was white.

I did Tamara's hair every morning, which tickled my friends of both races, who just couldn't believe that I, a white woman, could do a Black child's hair. It needed to be greased, sectioned off, braided, and decorated with colorful bands, ties, and barrettes. My own two daughters did not go neglected and got French braids and tails, all decorated as well. I made sure all the girls knew they were beautiful.

Tamara had been schooled to be guarded around white people. Once when she was curious about something I was drinking, I offered her a sip, and she hesitated. I asked her if her mother had told her not to drink out of the same glass as a white person and she sheepishly answered yes. I reassured her that was okay. She should always respect what her mother has told her, even when she was at our house. What mattered was that her mother and I both loved her. I tried not to put her in the same position I had put my children during the divorce.

Tamara's mother, who hadn't been in touch at all during this time, showed up unannounced one day to reclaim her daughter. Derek wasn't home. Tamara did not want to go. While I talked with her mother, my children helped her escape out their bedroom window and hide behind the building. I explained to Tamara's mother that I didn't feel comfortable letting Tamara go without her father being there. Jeremy popped into the room and announced that Tamara was playing over at someone else's house.

Her mother was a big, intimidating woman. I was frightened but tried not to show it as I backed her out of my apartment, assuring her she could discuss it all with Derek. She yielded. Her boyfriend, who was waiting on the porch, hit me so hard that I was knocked down by the blow. Then they left. When I told Derek about it later, he did not have the reaction I expected. Phil would have seen to it that they guy was hospitalized, or maybe disappeared altogether. Derek was not all that concerned. I was confused.

The next day, Derek made arrangements to return Tamara to her mother. I never saw her again.

I was in my living room holding my one-year-old when Derek's ex—a different ex, not Tamara's mother—burst in and smacked me in the head while the baby was still in my arms. I handed my little one off to his sister and launched myself on the intruder. I threw her face-down, climbed on top of her, and wrapped her hair around my hand. I pulled her head up and punched her in the face and then slammed her face down on the floor.

"Eat carpet, bitch!"

I screamed that. Again and again. It was as if I were in a blackout. Blacked out with rage.

Neighbors and their kids crowded my doorway, egging me on. I registered the voices of my children cheering. And stopped. She had violently invaded our home, but what were my children watching me do? I pulled her up and pushed her out the door. Halfway down the stairway she turned and yelled something, I don't remember what, but it was enough to make me leap over the stair rail to tackle her and start again. A pair of strong arms caught me from behind. Derek. I was so glad he stopped me. I was out of my mind.

After the fight I was notorious. People feared and respected me. My kids bragged about their mom. Nine-year-old Jeremy was especially proud of me, strutting around on my newfound reputation. I liked that my son admired me. A lot. Too much.

Jeremy stopped going outside. Indoors, he paced. When I sent him out to play, he said he couldn't.

"What do you mean you can't go outside?" I demanded.

One of the bigger boys had told him that the next time he saw him he would beat him up.

Most of the other women didn't like this boy's mother. The kid was a bully and she defended him. I didn't want my son to be a bully but wasn't going to let him be bullied either. I sent Jeremy outside and told him to stand up for himself. Within ten minutes, the two boys were fighting. I heard the other mother yell for her son to bite Jeremy. I raced down and snatched my son up. He was crying. He had tooth marks on his arm.

My friends were furious. They said I had to do something so the other mother didn't get away with this. I put the word out that she and I needed to meet and settle this once and for all. Emotions were high. I had a reputation for being no one to trifle with, but I felt strangely ashamed.

When that woman's son was losing the fight, she told him to bite my child. Who does that? Well, I might have. I have told my children that if they are in danger, they should bite, scratch, kick, or do anything necessary to defend themselves. The ones who deserved to be punished here were us mothers who had fought, as well as the mothers who encouraged fights in the first place, then watched, excited, when they went out of control.

We were the same group of mothers who, less than a month earlier, were out on our balconies at two o'clock in the morning, singing "We Are the World" while our children, who had been quiet indoors all day to escape the heat, were playing in the courtyard below. That heartfelt singing lifted us up in fellowship and mutual respect. Now the very same people were on their balconies sharing a different kind of fellowship while the two of us eyed each other from opposite sides of the courtyard. When we got close enough to hear each other without shouting, I asked her to stop a second.

"I really don't feel like entertaining the whole complex with this stupid fight, do you?" I asked her. "How 'bout we just go have coffee and figure this out?"

The look of relief I saw on her face put a look of relief on my own. She was a big woman, and probably would have kicked my ass, although neither one of us were really fighters. We were Moms. Moms with children for goodness sake. Where were our priorities? We went into my apartment and left them all outside wondering what was going on.

I made coffee. We talked about behavior in our courtyard, on the school playground and at the bus stop. There were other boys bullying her son. We had to make peace among ourselves and with the other moms, whether we liked each other or not. We couldn't tell the boys to be nice and then just keep on fighting with each other. We had to show them how to discuss things and work out their disagreements. We made a second pot of coffee. When we emerged, we were laughing. We became friends and so did our boys.

When Derek and I didn't have money to get high, we went cruising in my truck. Derek would get a bottle from the liquor store. I drank chocolate milk and drove.

Although things had calmed down inside the apartment complex, the altercation I'd had with Derek's ex was still simmering. We'd had a string of confrontations with various members of that family.

One night in the parking lot of a liquor store, one of them drove up. Derek jumped out, muttering about "gonna take care of this once and for all" and the two guys were immediately fighting. The other girlfriend and I sat in our respective trucks, me in the driver's seat, her in the passenger seat, face to face, headlights shining with the two in combat between us. I had one foot on the brake and one foot on the gas. In case I had to run somebody over, I thought.

Derek managed to get this guy up against the passenger door of the truck. The window was open. Derek's knife was sitting on the truck seat.

"Give it to me, Baby," he said.

I didn't hesitate.

The other guy must have seen because he yelled, "Baby, bring me my knife!"

She did.

I let my foot up off the brake a little. Ready to run her over. I was really thinking that.

Then the guy was on the ground, the woman on top of him screaming, the owner of the liquor store running towards them. Derek jumped in the truck.

"I stuck him! I stuck him and my dick got hard! Drive, Baby! Drive!"

Without hesitation, I drove.

Derek made a plan. I was to drop him off at the house of a friend who would find a place to stash him. Then I was to go home to the kids. He told me what to say to the cops. We slowed down next to a field where he tossed the two knives, his and the other guy's.

I drove home, trembling, and parked way down in the parking lot, away from where I usually do. I didn't wonder at all about who that other man might be. A father? A son? I didn't wonder if he was alive or dead. I put on my pajamas, hid my clothes, and got into bed. Soon enough, the knock came on the door.

I opened the door slowly, making my voice sound scratchy with sleep.

"Yes, Officer. Is there a problem?"

I let them in, yawning and rubbing my eyes.

One of the officers believed me. "You can tell she just got out of bed. I don't think it was her."

I thought I was going to fool them, but the other officer wasn't convinced.

"Where's your truck?"

"Derek has it."

"Where is he?"

"I don't know, probably with my truck—wait a minute! What's this all about? Has something happened to Derek? Was there an accident? What's going on?" I acted like I was getting a little angry.

"I think you'd better come with us. We need to talk."

They led me down the balcony. People were coming out of their apartments. I yelled to my next-door neighbor to watch my kids. She said she would, not to worry. *I have such good friends*, I thought.

At the police station, in a room with the two of them, I kept asking what happened. They responded with questions about my truck. It wasn't in its usual place, they said, but they knew where it was, so how did it get there?

"Am I being arrested?" I asked, still acting confused, and also, due to my law enforcement classes and PI experience, knowing my rights.

They said, they didn't want me. They pulled out a shirt that was so drenched in blood it was hard to tell it had ever been white.

"Do you know who this belongs to?

I remained silent.

Have you ever been to jail?"

I refused to answer.

They read me my rights and gave me a choice. I could help them out, or I could ask for an attorney.

I told them I wanted to help, but I was awfully sleepy right now so maybe I should just go home, get some sleep and come back later.

"That's what you want to do?" the angry cop demanded. "If you want to save that n—'s ass so much, you can fry with him."

It was morning by then. In the women's section of the jail, women were sitting or lying around. A TV was on. As soon as I was delivered, they started to ask questions. I wasn't sure how much I wanted them to know and was evasive. Someone insisted I tell them what I was charged with.

"Attempted murder?" *Had all this really happened?*

I crawled into my bunk. I missed my kids. I had no idea where Derek was or what was going to happen next. I was scared.

Because of the seriousness of my crime, no one gave me too much trouble or asked very many questions. I wasn't there on a drug crime, so that set me apart. Some of the girls were nice. Most of them were addicts. I spent most of my first days in jail on the pay phone trying to get information about my kids. On one of those calls, a neighbor told me the police were in my house at that very moment. I demanded to speak with an officer and told him that they had no permission to be there and had to leave immediately. They did. I thought about the bloody shirt under the towels in the linen cupboard and was scared.

After a few days in jail, I heard Derek had been arrested. He had been to prison before and knew the ropes, so we were quickly communicating daily with "kites." Inmates who had been there the longest and proven themselves became trustees. They had jobs around the jail, in the cafeteria, mopping floors, etc. If you wanted to communicate with another inmate, you wrote a letter, folded it up into a small triangle, a "kite," and gave it to a trustee. The trustee would "fly" it to its destination. Derek and I wrote daily. I figured out a schedule for talking on the phone with my kids. Jail life became bearable.

I was on my way to the phones when I saw a large Hispanic woman, a known fighter, that the other women were afraid of. She was sobbing. She loved her man so much she got arrested in his place and was doing his time. He didn't love her. He had someone else now. No one would ever love her. She would be alone the rest of her life and just wanted to die and get it over with.

Words about God began flowing out of me, how He has loved her all along and with that love she would never be alone. I had never had a conversation like that with anyone before, but the words just poured out. "We can reach out to Him right now," I told her. We prayed together. I felt the presence of God. She became more peaceful. So did I.

Someone in the block received a kite from a family member of the guy who had been stabbed. He was badly injured but would recover. The women whispered and threw me looks. I was in danger. There were so many ways and so many places I could get hurt. In the cafeteria line, I inserted myself behind my new friend. I tapped her on the shoulder and asked her if she had my back.

"I gotcha," she said.

I was safe.

I heard my name over the loudspeakers. Then the announcement. Not that I had a visitor or a package, but, "CPS has your children. "

I screamed. The other girls moaned at what a heartless way that was to tell me. Hadn't I talked with my kids every day? Didn't the neighbors assure me they were okay? I had been optimistic about my situation until then, chatty with everyone, even the guards, making the most out of my outgoing personality. When I heard that I lost my children, I withdrew and refused to speak, even at the order of a guard. Finally, at a hearing, I spoke for the first time in weeks.

I told the judge that I needed to restore my family. I assured him I was not a flight risk. I had four kids, so anywhere I went, I would have to be on welfare, and could be tracked down. He believed me and let me out of jail.

I found a motel I could afford in the Sacramento neighborhood of Oak Park. It was full of low-income people, many of them doing drugs. It had a swimming pool. One of the rooms had a lot of men living in it. They were cocaine addicts, Black men who spotted my biracial son and thought I was easy pickings. They saw I was alone and started giving me problems. I wrote Derek about it. He sent a friend to talk to them. They became polite and never bothered me after that. It felt so good to know I'd found a man who would take care of me like that. Soon we would be reunited. My life was turning back into a fairy tale come true.

Derek had made a friend in jail who said that the kids and I could live with his wife and son in a large house by the river. It was an old three-story Victorian house that looked like a mansion. It was beautiful on the outside but trashed on the inside, with falling-down ceilings in some of the rooms. We found a room that was free of debris with two mattresses on the floor and called it ours. We cuddled together under borrowed blankets. When the kids fell asleep, I turned out the light and heard the rats climbing between the walls. It sounded like there were hundreds of them. I sat up all night with the light on and a shoe in my hand ready to defend my children.

I wrote Derek every day and visited on days it was allowed. I saved his letters and read them over and over. The children were having fun. There were trees to climb, and toys to play with in the yard. They even had a goat. Inside the house there was an old pool table and Jeremy soon mastered the game. I became friends with the wife of Derek's friend. We had a lot in common and many stories to trade. I never found out what her husband was in jail for, but the seriousness of our crime made him do whatever Derek wanted.

When Derek's friend got out of jail, everything changed. It became apparent we weren't welcome, but he was afraid to make Derek mad. The friend was abusive to his wife, verbally and physically, especially when he drank. He forbade her to speak to me if he wasn't there. He was probably afraid I would convince her to leave him. I certainly would have tried.

Finally, Derek was released. When he saw our living situation, he packed us up and we moved. We spent the next week or so living in the car.

Derek found us a small, one bedroom, second floor apartment full of cockroaches and drug use, which fit us just fine. It was cheap, and the landlord did not care what we did. At that time, we weren't using every day. Some of the neighbors were nice, and fun to talk to. We spent most of our time out in the small parking lot, Derek playing bones (dominoes) on the hood of our station wagon. The people who sold me that car didn't have a title. When I couldn't get tags for it, Jeremy went out one night and stole some. I thanked him.

After Derek had been out playing bones for hours, I would bring him a plate of fried potatoes and sausage, one of the three dishes I knew how to cook.

The other guys would demand, "Hey where's ours?"

Derek would fire back, "Get your own woman to cook for you."

It made me feel so proud. My life was taking shape.

Derek was washing down the parking lot and driveway one day. From the window I saw his ex—yet another ex—out there flirting with him. I flew outside, enraged.

"Let me wash this trash out the drive." I said, grabbing the hose.

"Don't you get one drop...." She started to yell but could not finish the sentence because I shoved the hose down her throat. Water went everywhere. Then I was on top of her, hitting her with my fists and shoving her face into the pavement, over and over until I was exhausted.

"Get me up" I hollered to Derek, who was standing there watching, grinning. He helped me to my feet. I had been clenching my jaw so tight that I broke a tooth. His ex lay there panting. I was glad she didn't come after me because I couldn't have fought any more.

I heard stories of how badly she was messed up. She'd been seen in the store, holding a towel to cover her face as she shopped. Derek was very proud. She never came around again. What I couldn't get out of my head was the memory of Derek watching and grinning. How many exes did he have? Were they actually "ex?" Was he provoking these fights?

I told Derek that if he hit me again, he'd better kill me because if he didn't, I would find a way to kill him. I didn't want our relationship to end. My kids, especially Jeremy, were attached to him. I liked how it felt to be with such a well-respected and strong man. I thought my threat was going to protect me from the worst of his rages. I had shown him many times that I could do the things that tough people do.

I remember a particular day, but I do not remember what we were arguing about. Probably a sudden and unplanned absence or maybe the exes who continued to turn up. We were in bed, me between him and the wall. He kept asking me if I wanted him to leave. Finally I said yes.

I felt the sting of the wall on my face harder than his hand on the back of my head. My nose hurt. Broken. Yet another spatter of blood on the wall.

He slammed out of the apartment. I started throwing his clothes out the window, down to where he was yelling up at me from the parking lot. He left when the neighbors came out. One couple invited me to come to their apartment where I would be safe. (Where were my children? I don't remember.) A while later he knocked on the door and they let him in. I ran into the bathroom. (Hadn't I learned not to do that?) He pounded on the door as I sat, back to the wall, with my feet pressed against it. Despite my attempts to block it, the door crashed around my legs. He yanked me out into the living room, where I curled up into a ball with my head covered. The neighbors watched while he kicked me. I heard voices begging him to stop. Nobody called for help. They were too scared of Derek.

I saw the open front door out the corner of my eye and ran for it. My friends and neighbors followed as I stumbled down the stairs. There were seven men and eight women. No one even dared hold Derek back. I knew the keys were in the car, so I dashed to it, jumped in, and started backing out. Next I saw Derek near the front fender, lifting a rock the size of a large baby over his head. I stepped on the gas. He tossed the rock through the windshield. It landed on the seat next to me. I jumped out. He grabbed me and threw me against the back of the station wagon.

"She told me if I ever hit her, I'd have to kill her," he shouted to the onlookers behind him. "Or else she'll kill me."

As I slid off the car, I saw the dent that my ass had made in the tailgate.

Once I hit the ground I could no longer move. My face landed in a puddle, but I could not lift it out. He kicked me. I heard the sound and felt myself bounce but had no feeling. I could no longer see. Voices screamed for him to stop. Someone was crying.

The police were there. Lights flashed.

"Go help her, " someone said.

"What happened? Did anybody see anything?" the cop asked. No answer.

"Come on man, you can see her laying there, help her!" A male voice this time.

"Nobody saw anything? She must not need help."

I tasted the mud seeping into my mouth.

"Since nothing happened, I guess we'll go."

"I saw it!" The male voice again. "For the love of God, I saw it!"

The police radio crackled. They told the ambulance waiting in front of the building to come. I lay in the mud, unable to move. They escorted Derek away.

I spent a night in the hospital and came home hurting, afraid, and wanting only one thing—Phil. Yes,

Phil. I know it sounds crazy and of course it is. I needed protection, which to me meant having a man in my house to keep me safe. It only took a couple of phone calls to find him. He was still in Reno. He had always hated the idea of IV drugs, so telling him how Derek had started me on cocaine was enough. Two days later I was at the station, meeting his bus.

As we walked back to the apartment together, he told me about his life in Reno in the months since I left, particularly his association with a woman who dealt cards at one of the casinos, how she was so beautiful and wore diamonds in her fingernails. He brought me gifts he had probably stolen from her. He set a framed picture of her next to his side of the bed.

From the very first day, Phil impressed my neighbors with his drinking and storytelling. He could walk into a store wearing a black trench coat and come out with bottles of whiskey in every pocket. They loved him. Jeremy was so glad to see him.

One day I came home after shopping and found all the letters that Derek had written me from jail spread out on the bed. I got mad. We argued. He walked out. I took scissors to the diamond-fingernail girl's picture, cut it up in little pieces and threw them out the window into the parking lot like confetti. Strangely, he seemed to like that. The fight fizzled out. I thought that by taking such a fearless risk, I had gained his respect.

Soon, I discovered that I was pregnant. Although there had been some doubt as to whether or not Phil was the father of my last baby, this time there was no question. I was giving Phil his baby. This would cement our relationship for sure.

Phil surprised me one day with cocaine. I couldn't believe it at first. But as he got it ready, he chatted about how even though he preferred to smoke it, he was always good at hitting other people. I was confused. Wasn't he adamantly against doing cocaine the IV way? There was also no way I could turn it down. He gave me the hit and I fell back into the bliss, higher than I could remember. Suddenly he was in my face, shouting about how awful I was for saying yes to this, how I'd better give it up.

I didn't understand why he was doing this to me. It was dangerous to ruin someone's high that way. You could shock them into cardiac arrest. And he knew it.

Then he became even more affectionate than usual, showing me yoga positions and playfully twisting me into different shapes, telling me it was healthy to stretch. He pulled me over the foot of the bed. I asked what he was doing. He smiled gently and told me to relax, that he wanted to try something. He bent me further and further until I felt a tearing in my abdomen. I cried for him to stop and he helped me up. The cramping and bleeding started a few days later. As the paramedics came to take me to the hospital for yet another D&C, Phil watched from the kitchen.

Phil drank heavily with the neighbors, often blacking out. I discovered that if I got myself good and drunk first, guzzling straight from a bottle sometimes to be more efficient about it, Phil would slow his drinking to take care of me. I was a demanding drunk, the kind who threw weepy tantrums, wailed for food, and carried on about how awful my life had been. This prompted Phil to console and reassure me which I liked a lot.

I have a woozy memory of him tossing me over one shoulder and heading up the outside flight of stairs that led to our apartment, aware that everyone was impressed with his strength. I relaxed into it, flopping like a doll. Instead of tucking me lovingly into bed, he sat me down on the couch and punched me square in the face, breaking my nose yet again.

The rest I only remember in flashes. Me screaming in the living room. Me in the bedroom reassuring the crying children, telling them to stay put. Somehow, I was back in the living room getting beat up again. Still later I woke up on the bed, my face swollen and blood-encrusted and Phil sitting next to me cleaning his rifle. He slowly loaded it, explaining that he was going to have to kill me.

"But the children…"

He interrupted. "I'm going to have to kill them, too."

I had to get Phil out of the apartment.

I jumped up, ran to the door, turned, and yelled, "Then kill me you fucking punk!" Nothing set Phil off faster than being called a punk, a term that was prison code for being somebody's bitch. I walked away slowly without turning around. I felt so calm, knowing that a rifle shot was about to blow through the back of my head.

I reached the bottom of the stairs without being blown apart and panicked. He hadn't followed me and instead was in that apartment with a loaded rifle, alone with my kids. I ducked out of the courtyard, heading for the front of the building and ran straight into the arms of a police officer. "He's up there with my kids and he has a gun!"

Outside on the street were several police cars, lights flashing. The officer guided me behind his car and told me to stay low. I got on my hands and knees, and then realized that the car was rolling towards me. I started crawling backwards, yelling for the officer, who cried "Oh shit!" and jumped into the rolling car, jerking it to a stop just as Phil came around the corner of the building.

Picture a muscled black man, a former Mr. Las Vegas, with his hands in the air, wearing nothing but red bikini briefs, awkwardly running on bare feet and shouting, "Trish! Trish! I love you!"

An officer pointed to his underwear and shouted, "The gun! The gun!"

I knew he didn't have a gun in there—that was all Phil. I yelled for them not to shoot while he continued shouting his love for me. The officers backed him up against the front wall of the apartment building. Phil looked straight at me. Suddenly I was terrified, not for myself and my children, but for Phil. One of the officers put his hand down Phil's underwear, frisking him.

"Suck my dick motherfucker!" he shouted. Then he was laughing.

I sat down hard on the pavement. One eye was swollen shut. I wheezed through my bloody broken nose and hurt all over. Some officers took Phil away. Two others escorted me back up the stairs to my apartment to my children who were unharmed but confused and crying.

Jeremy told me the rest of what had happened. While I was in the living room getting beat up, he had thrown a mattress out the upstairs window, jumped down on to it, then ran to the corner pay phone and called the police. He was terrified in doing that, because he was sure that if the police came Phil would get shot. But he was also terrified that if the police didn't come, Phil would kill me. I told him he was a hero. He was nine years old.

Later that night some people from a church showed up and talked to me. I was exhausted, hurting, and in shock, so most of what they said washed over me without registering. One of them, a well-groomed young man, looked me straight in the eye and said God had told him that there was something special I was going to do, and that I needed to stay alive so I could do it. I wanted that to be true, but it was hard to believe.

The next morning, which was only a few hours later, the door exploded off its hinges and landed in the middle of the kitchen floor. Phil.

"You called the cops on me!" he shouted.

He was wearing clothes that were way too small and looked ridiculous. I raised a shoe to hit him with. When he saw my two black eyes, swollen nose, and split lip he started crying and telling me how sorry he was. He promised he would do anything to make it up to me. I backed him up to the bedroom window with the shoe and made him jump out like my son had had to do. He agreed to get help. We went to our first AA meeting that very day.

I sat in a chair, numb, rocking back and forth. I could sense people looking at me but didn't look up. Despite the ice packs, my whole face was still swollen, one eye shut and the other blackened. My lips were too puffy for me to form coherent words. They asked me if I wanted to speak. I just kept rocking. I felt humiliated and ashamed. So Phil spoke.

"She's my wife!" he cried. "I love her and look what I've done to her!"

Phil went on and on about how sorry he was, how he didn't ever want to hurt me again, how he would do anything because he didn't want to lose me. He didn't mention anything about his alcohol problem. I thought that was the reason why we were there. Instead, it felt like he was showing me off like a trophy.

The men took him to another room to get coffee and talk some more. The women did the same with me. They were beautiful and spoke to me like I mattered, saying I had to do whatever it took so that this never happened again.

What was I supposed to do? How could I get him to stop drinking? He was the one with the drinking problem. I only drank to keep him from drinking his way to a blackout, so if he got his drinking under control, I wouldn't need to drink anymore. He was the one who had beat me up. Now I was the one who had to make sure he didn't do it again? Were these women trying to tell me to leave him? Was I supposed to just throw our love away? Didn't we come here so we could stay together? They brought up the children who had witnessed everything. Could this have hurt them? The children loved Phil. These people didn't know him. They didn't know us.

Phil was sorry for what he had done. He admitted that he was the one with the problem. He had promised to do whatever he had to do. I started going to Al-Anon, group meetings for people who have a family member with an alcohol problem. Phil never went to another meeting. It took another broken nose before we finally separated.

I liked being sober. The things I heard in Al-Anon meetings made sense to me. You can't prevent another person from behaving badly, people said. I learned that alcohol could destroy people's lives. I got a sponsor that I could call any time. I didn't tell anyone about the cocaine.

Jeremy started to complain that everything was boring and stupid. Our outings were "just for little kids." He was disruptive in school because it was "dumb." I met with his teachers and tried to convince them that his mischief came from a lack of challenging work to do. Special work would come, they said, when he demonstrated that he could behave. They wanted him to take Ritalin and I refused, though I did cut sugar and processed foods from his diet.

In a fundamental way that I never understood, Jeremy believed that if he wanted something he deserved to have it. He stole some collectable cards from the desk of a student and the child's mother came to my door asking to have them back. I was humiliated, but Jeremy was furious to have to give them up. I tried to spend more time alone with just him. Nothing was working. He missed Gordie.

My roommate moved out. I couldn't afford the rent by myself. I, too, was homesick for Spokane. So I made a down payment on a Dodge Colt with no intention of making any of the payments. I packed as much of our stuff as would fit in it, left the rest behind, and headed back to Spokane, hoping to move in with my parents until I could get my feet on the ground. Mama made it clear that her grandchildren were welcome to stay with her, but I was not. My sister wouldn't speak to me.

4. Downward Spiral

I reconnected with Alice. She invited me to stay with her and was relaxed about the kids. They seemed to enjoy camping out on her floor and were happy to be back in Spokane. Alice and I played cards, drank, and made flirting phone calls to guys on the Air Force base nearby. All you had to do was call any 244 number and you'd be talking to somebody. Sometimes the guys came over to play cards. Many times they stayed. That's how I met Alan.

Our whirlwind romance started as soon as we met. Alan was divorced and his two teenage kids lived with their mother in Portland. He wanted everything that I did—a modest home, a loving family, and a relationship with God. My kids loved him. We went house-hunting and started spending time with my parents. When I broke my collarbone in a freak accident, he loaned me his car for a week because it was an automatic, easier to drive than my Dodge Colt.

One day while I was out, a woman came looking for me. She told Alice she got my name and address from some paperwork she had found on the floor of her car. Not only did she and her two kids live in base housing, she and Alan were very much married. Alan denied everything the next time he came over, but I wouldn't even let him out of the car.

"You made me trash!" I screamed at him.

I was devastated. For a day or two. I wasn't a sit-around-and-mope kind of girl. I went right back out to look for someone new. Believe me, there were plenty of them out there.

I was on my way home from grocery shopping, in my little Dodge Colt with my three youngest kids and the dog, when a big blue Thunderbird ran a red light and T-boned us. The impact sent us flying across the intersection and we landed inches away from a tele-phone pole. Apparently, I dove in front of the two kids in the passenger seat, because when I came to and sat back in front of the steering wheel, I saw strands of my hair dangling from the broken glass of the windshield on the passenger side.

I heard the soothing voices of my angels, reciting in unison, "The kids are OK. Everything is all right."

The youngest, just over two years old, was screaming. I mimicked the comforting tone of my angels and spoke calmly to the children. I asked them to relax and feel their bodies with their minds, starting with their heads and moving slowly down to their toes.

"Tell me if anything hurts," I said. They were quiet.

I turned towards the two children next to me and saw the face of my youngest covered in blood. And screamed.

We all went to the hospital, but nobody had to stay.

As a result of the accident, we were awarded enough money to get settled in a little house on the Southeast side, buy a used pick-up truck and a used Ford Capri, which was very nice. We also bought furniture, a TV and stereo and a fully stocked aquarium, all for our new house. In addition, I bought the kids clothes and toys. Everything was used, but charming. The most important thing is that no one had been hurt in the accident. I was grateful for God's protection

Alice and I started going dancing at clubs, leaving ten-year-old Jeremy in charge of my three other kids and Alice's two. That's how I met Carl. He was extremely good looking, kind of the Denzel Washington type, though aside from my dancing skills, I saw no reason why he, a lieutenant in the Air Force, would want to be with me. He took me out for breakfast at one of the all-night diners. There, he took my hand and examined my badly chewed hot pink nails.

"If you want to be with me," he said, "this is not acceptable." I began taking better care of my nails.

We went to his apartment that night. He insisted on using a rubber—a sock, he called it. He already had a child in Florida. It wouldn't be good for his Air Force career if he had another without being married— which I took as a signal that he was interested in marriage, which in turn made me giddy because he was so far out of my league, so polite and so generous with compliments. Whenever he called, I would come over and spend the night.

He told me about his plans to march and attend a celebration downtown for Martin Luther King Day, then a relatively new holiday. I had attended the festivities the year before with Alice and was pleased at the prospect of going with him. No, he said forcefully. As a white person, I wouldn't be welcome there. I went with Alice instead. Carl spotted us in the crowd and turned away when I waved. Alice said that was concerning, but I made some lame excuse for his behavior.

I went on seeing Carl for several more months, until it became clear even to me that our encounters weren't anything more than booty calls. He was always prepared, with plenty of "socks," and would drive me home right after. I was flattered that he wanted to be with me at all. Only once did I ever sit on the couch in his living room. He offered me the remotes to his sound system and TV and told me to make myself at home. I felt awkward and out of place, like I didn't belong in this man's life, only his bed.

One night the rubber broke and of course, four weeks later I discovered I was pregnant. He was in anguish. To my surprise, he did not get mad or blame me in anyway. He just didn't want me to have this baby and offered me $85,000 to have an abortion.

I already had four kids. He argued that I did not need another one nearly as much as I needed $85,000. It would have changed my life. It would have given my children different kinds of chances. He wouldn't continue to see me if I didn't accept his offer. Everyone I knew told me to do it.

I have never regretted saying no.

The pregnancy progressed. My family had no interest in the coming baby. Alice, and another friend named Rashaad helped me out a lot. They brought over food and stayed with my kids when I had to go to doctor's appointments.

Because I was high risk, I had many ultrasounds, so we knew it would be a girl. Jeremy said we had enough girls in the family already and decided he should be getting a little brother. If someone mentioned the new baby with the pronoun "she," Jeremy would correct them. I tried to explain, as gently as I could, that it wasn't possible to change the doctor's findings. He would hear none of it and yelled that he hated his sisters, and all girls were stupid. Little pink dresses and nighties and blankets began to accumulate.

In order to get Jeremy more involved in the pregnancy, I took him out to an abandoned parking lot and taught him to drive the pick-up. If the baby came too early and too fast, I would count on him to drive me to the hospital. I arranged with the doctors so he could be present when she came into the world. All this excited him enough to get him looking forward to the birth. Once again, I found myself confined to bed for the last months of pregnancy. Unbeknownst to me, Jeremy was stealing bicycles, dismantling them, reassembling them differently, and selling them.

My labor started six weeks early, just before dawn on Jeremy's eleventh birthday. When I woke him up, he flew out of bed, excited at the prospect of driving, though I told him that I was able to manage it. He threw a bicycle in the back and hopped in. He made sure everyone at the hospital knew it was his birthday.

The labor was intense, as labors go. The baby was surprisingly large for being so early. Jeremy whooped with excitement when the wonderful moment came. Everyone was astounded. A baby boy.

Jeremy grabbed his bicycle from the truck in the parking garage and rode all the way home with the news. Friends were calling one another asking if the baby was really a boy. Meanwhile, I was fighting for my life.

I had been laying on my right side and when I rolled over, I felt a large mass in my belly that stayed behind. I grabbed a nurse and put her hand on my side. My uterus was filling with blood. The nurse offered to give me something for the pain, but I declined feebly, wanting to keep my milk safe and natural. The nurse shushed me and promised there was no way I was going to endure what was about to happen without painkillers. The doctor then went up to his elbow inside me, grasping for my womb. The room was filled with people rushing about giving orders and repeating them back to each other. Somebody asked me if I minded a blood transfusion. I didn't care. I fell unconscious.

When I woke up, a nurse told me that I was going to be okay, the baby was okay, my kids were okay, and I had a visitor. Daddy. What was he doing there? Who called him? He said he came because he heard I might die. I'm still surprised that he had seemed to care whether I had lived or died.

I slept for 24 hours. When I woke, I finally got to nurse my little boy, look into his eyes, and say hello. He looked like his father. Beautiful eyes, black hair. But what was his name? I had only considered girls' names. It took a while before I could name my little boy.

Like many preemies, he was jaundiced and had to be under a lamp for several days. The doctors kept me in the hospital as well, so we both went home together. Friends scrambled to get little boy things.

The baby was such a joy, never fussy. His thoughts connected with me. He would lie beside me and look at me. I could sense him saying "Feed me," so calm and strong. None of the other children did that. He had the blackest belly button I had ever seen, and soon we all stopped using his name and called him "Brownie Buttons."

A year later, I had to stop nursing because I discovered that I was pregnant again. I was seeing two different guys at the time and didn't know who the father was. One said he had been poisoned with Agent Orange in Desert Storm and couldn't have children. (Agent Orange was not used in Desert Storm, it was used only in Vietnam.) The other one only came by occasionally. But it only takes once.

Meanwhile, Jeremy had gotten arrested and taken to Juvenile Hall for stealing motorcycles. A hearing was scheduled to determine whether he should come home or spend more time there. The public defender reported that the prosecutor was agreeable to him coming home, but with certain conditions. On the day of the hearing, the kids begged not to go to daycare. I expected to be gone an hour or two. My nine-year-old daughter was confident she could manage the baby. I left them snacks, reminded them where the emergency numbers were, and promised I would call them from the courthouse.

Gordie, who had never taken an interest in Jeremy's problems, was already at the courthouse when I got there. He was all decked out in the uniform of his new job with the Postal Service and looked very official. He didn't speak to me but had plenty to say to the judge who was very interested in his point of view. Gordie called Jeremy incorrigible, said he was a danger to society and should be incarcerated indefinitely. The hearing dragged on for four hours.

Witnesses described Jeremy's history, painted him to be a career criminal. It seemed like I was the only one on Jeremy's side.

At every break in the hearing, I called home, explaining the delays and checking to make sure everything was ok. The baby had messed in his pants and his sister said she couldn't get him clean—would he be ok till I got home? I said I thought so but offered to come home if she wanted me to. She said they were okay. If I didn't stay, no one would speak on behalf of Jeremy.

The understanding between the public defender and the prosecutor was swept aside and the judge ordered more time. I left feeling defeated and arrived home to a house surrounded by flashing lights. Police cars, a fire truck. I raced inside, panicked. My daughter greeted me at the door, crying. A woman immediately put herself between us, stuck out her hand and introduced herself. Janet Baxter. Terrified, I asked her what had happened, where my other children were, who had been hurt. She peppered me with questions, personal questions. She wanted to know about my family, where I had been, and why I had left my children alone.

When I realized no one had been hurt, I was even more bewildered about what was happening. Janet Baxter called Mama. I was relieved. Mama would be able to tell this woman whatever it was she wanted to know. I overheard the woman saying, "Believe me, I understand, I have a daughter just like her." I focused on changing the baby and reassuring the other children that everything was going to be ok, which was hard, because I was so frightened myself.

Meanwhile the police were searching the house, the shed, and my vehicles, ransacking everything. What were they looking for? I hadn't used cocaine since I left Sacramento. They trashed my house and found nothing.

Janet Baxter commented to the police, disgusted, "That baby looks like its diaper hasn't been changed in months."

My daughter hadn't cleaned him up perfectly, but there was no diaper rash, not even redness. I had five children. I knew how to take care of a baby.

They took my children to the living room. Janet Baxter sat me down in the kitchen and told me that arrangements had been made for me and my children to stay with my parents for a while. That made no sense to me, but she repeated that it had been decided. I didn't think to ask her who had decided this. Nor did it occur to me to find out who had called her in the first place.

The woman said that I should gather my things and meet her and the children at my parents' house. When I got there, the place was empty and dark. Only later, sitting in my parents' dim living room, would I get through on the phone to the CPS office and find out that Janet Baxter had taken my children straight there where she met Gordie and my parents. There was no need for me to come down. My daughters had gone to live with their father. My parents would be keeping my two younger boys.

At home, alone, I paced through the empty, ransacked rooms yelling at God.

"Why? I demanded. "You motherfucker! Why have you done this to me?"

For just an instant the house grew darker. For the first time in my life, I sensed anger from God. I did not understand.

I believed that my life was in God's control. It was God who raised me, saw me through my childhood, my marriage, my relationships. He got me through the empty, scary nights. He got me safe through all the dangerous pregnancies and presented me with all those beautiful children. He was sending these men into my life.

I greeted every new relationship with a prayer, asking God if this man was the one for me. If he wasn't, I asked God to end the relationship quickly because I was willing to continue looking until I found the man who would make me feel safe and happy. I demanded that God show me why He had put me through all this. I blamed Him for everything.

The only relationship I counted on was now in jeopardy because of my rage. The pain I felt was all-consuming, worse than any beating. I was confused, scared, and more alone than I had ever felt.

There was no way I was ever going to please Janet Baxter, the Spokane CPS worker. She had no concerns about my high-risk pregnancy. She thought I had enough kids already. Once, during one of her many surprise visits to my house, the guy I was seeing walked in without knocking with a big grin on his face. He asked if I needed anything. He was polite and respectful.

After he left, she waved at my belly and sneered, "Is this baby's daddy Black too?"

At first, I had the impression that she might agree that this was all a misunderstanding and let my children come home. But she started raising objections. She said I had too many children for the size of my house. The house was tiny, almost a cottage, but she described it to the judge as "more of a lean too than an actual house."

I had the city of Spokane inspect my home. The inspector was nice, called it cute and cozy. He testified that it met all requirements for single parent household with four children. But it wasn't good enough for Janet Baxter, because nothing would ever be good enough for Janet Baxter.

I moved a block away into a duplex with two big bedrooms. I transported almost everything in my children's red wagon. I was able to borrow a pickup truck to take our beds and mattresses.

We had our visits at CPS. I became friendly with Franklin, a foster parent whose foster child visited his mom there at the same time I visited my kids. He was the assistant pastor at a church and invited me to attend.

The first time I went, I knew that I belonged there. Tears ran down my face as the pastor spoke directly to my pain. He explained how Jesus, more than anyone, understood what it means to suffer, and how even our most despicable deeds wouldn't cause God to stop loving us. I was as if God was speaking through him. Perhaps I had not been abandoned by God after tall.

Franklin and I became great friends. Just friends. He became an unofficial godfather to my children. When, once again, I was confined to bed for the last months of the pregnancy, his encouragement on the phone was the first thing I heard in the morning and the last thing I heard at night. He helped me find rides to doctor's appointments, to church, and to the visits with my children. When my beautiful daughter was born, six weeks early, he was there in the delivery room. She had black curly hair and huge black eyes that charmed everyone. I dressed her in clothes trimmed with lace and put little bows in her hair.

My life had love and purpose again.

The whole congregation adored her. The women competed for the right to hold her. They all knew my story—my childhood, the disastrous relationships, all the unfairness I bumped into with my biracial family. I became the lead soprano in the choir, a speck of vanilla in an otherwise Black church.

Cleotha was the pianist and choir director for the church. Music was our bond. She used to dance for Quincy Jones and could play any song after hearing it once. Her living room was essentially a jam room, with piano keyboard, drums, and sound system. I spent hours with her there. Singing was how I prayed. My confidence grew.

I jumped through all the CPS hoops. I went to group sessions and classes. I let them observe me with my children. The counselors could not find anything wrong with me. Then my baby girl had to be hospitalized with RSV, a common respiratory virus in children which can be deadly for preemies. It was so hard to leave her there, under a tent. I was exhausted and bereft. I met a guy that used IV cocaine. Soon I was using again.

When I went to the hospital to visit my baby girl, she wanted to nurse, but I couldn't let her. My milk was poisoned. I told the staff that I was too tired to maintain my milk and do all the other things I had to do for the system. They gave her a bottle. She didn't want it. She didn't understand. She tried so hard to nurse and I had to keep pushing her away. Refusing her felt so terrible that I stayed away from the hospital. My beautiful little baby girl who had given my life meaning again. I let her down. Janet Baxter took her away. She said I couldn't hope to get her back unless I went to rehab. So I did.

After rehab, I moved into Cleotha's house. In exchange for rent, I received a home with music and a family.

Coming out of treatment the first time I was numb, on that pink cloud I had heard talk of in meetings. I rode the bus back and forth to the Twelve Step Club where I could hang out with clean and sober people. I went to Alcoholics Anonymous, and then discovered Narcotics Anonymous and Co-dependents Anonymous. I gobbled information and learned about myself in ways I'd never considered. I found a beautiful, kind woman to be my sponsor. Janet Baxter held my children in front of me like a carrot in front of a donkey. I wanted them back. I did everything I was told. After multiple court appearances and home inspections, they gave the kids to Gordie. I had believed them for months, but they were never going to forgive me.

I worked the program. But in my head was another, stronger program, the one I had heard for as long as I could remember: I was *worthless* and *bad* and would always be that way. Daddy was right. I would never be able to do anything. When I looked in the mirror, all I saw were the mistakes I had made. I deserved punishment. This wasn't humility. It was shame.

Only if I got my kids back, would my life be worth anything.

Jeremy, who was old enough to choose which parent to live with, chose me. He was already experimenting with alcohol and pot. He watched me go to meetings. Sometimes he went with me and listened to people talk about recovery all day long. We were a team, staying sober together. He charmed the older people with his smile and good manners. He was striking, twelve years old and already six feet tall. We went to clean-and-sober dances together and only danced with each other. I didn't want to dance with any of the men there. The girls were always flirting with Jeremy. He looked so much older than he was. I did my best to keep them away from him.

Then some trouble he had gotten into the last time I was using caught up with him—another incident involving motorcycles. He went to Juvenile Detention.

When the two girls visited me, they went to clubs and meetings, too. They played pinochle in leagues. The older one was nicknamed "Little Trish" by church grandmothers because we looked so much alike.

At home, the children were told that I was too far gone and would never change.

I started going to NAACP meetings with Cleotha, where I was the only white person in attendance. I would have been unwelcome if it hadn't been for Cleotha's authority. I might have looked like an interloper, but I was there because the issues of concern to this group directly affected my children.

We took on the police chief. He had come from Portland and was supposed to be an expert on gangs, but according to his reputation, he was cruel and unfair.

The Chief came to a meeting. I sat next to Cleotha. When he stopped speaking and opened up for questions, silence fell. I waited and waited, but no one asked a question. So I raised my hand and asked one. Soon the two of us were having a conversation, but everything he said was lame. I think he felt comfortable talking to a white person and assumed I would be lame just like he was.

My questions addressed specific problems his police force was causing among Spokane minorities— Black people, Native Americans, Hispanics, gays, low-income people, and single mothers. I asked his opinion about why 99% of Spokane's jail population was Black when only 2% of the city's population was. Why was the single black police officer on the force deployed to predominantly white neighborhoods instead of the southeast side where he might be sensitive to the people's needs? I slipped up and called him by the nickname that the neighborhood had given him. The crowd cheered. I had lots of friends that night. I made Cleotha proud.

Fueled by that evening, I attended a meeting organized by prominent citizens who thought the city of Spokane needed a Human Rights Commission. I was assigned to the Needs Committee, a group that collected complaints from the community. I spent hours and days on the phone, listening to stories from all over town. Some people spoke through tears, others in anger, all of them in frustration. They reported problems with the police department, land-lords, schools, businesses, and even churches.

The city council was not impressed with our findings. Even though Spokane was the only town of its size in the Northwest which didn't have a Human Rights Commission, the council denied that there was a race problem and suggested we were stirring up trouble where there had been none before. At the meeting where we presented information about all the complaints we gathered, I spoke calmly into the micro-phone. All eyes were locked on me. People listened. The mayor began to favor the idea of the commission.

Meanwhile our own pro-commission group split over how much power a Human Rights Commission should have. Many wanted the commission to have a lot of authority to step into situations and demand investigations. Others, myself included, thought that with so much resistance from the city council, getting a commission established was the most important thing, even if it involved making a few concessions. Cleotha didn't agree with me. It was hard to be at odds with my friend. I worried that I might be less welcome in her circle. In the end, they established a one-person commission and hired a Black female attorney to run it.

After that, I became known for my ability to fight the system and became an advocate for people of all sorts. My law enforcement classes had taught me that in every situation a person has rights, even if society looks down on people like them. I helped a pregnant woman in jail get the care she needed and advocated for immigrants who were getting cheated out of their wages. I am proud to have done all that, but other parts of my life shine much brighter in many people's memory

After I had been sober for about six months, my two older girls came to live with me again. All the way up until the court hearing when they were returned to me, Gordie harassed me. A phone call from him could send Janet Baxter out to my house for a surprise inspection. Once she found a garbage bag full of aluminum cans that the kids had collected for spending money when they visited. She argued that it was proof of how much I was drinking. I was proud of my children for being so independent. She twisted that around and called it neglect. In the hearing, Gordie admitted to some tactics that he called "discipline." He hit the three-year old in the head when she misbehaved. When Jeremy visited him, he sometimes threw him onto the bed and pinned him there until he agreed to what Gordie wanted. If it wasn't for that, I wouldn't have gotten them back.

Having the girls with me was as delightful as ever. We picked up where we left off. I walked them to the bus stop in the morning and met them there in the afternoon. We took ourselves on bus-riding adventures all over Spokane. Once again, a favorite place to explore was Riverfront Park. At home, we sang and danced to Bette Midler and Aretha Franklin. We planned a vacation and started saving for it.

I kept going to meetings and stayed sober. Everybody, including me, knew that I should never do cocaine again. Nor should I drink alcohol. Nobody, including me, focused on my primary addiction, the one born from the black hole in my heart. Relationships were my gateway drug. When a man pledged to love me forever (usually after we had been acquainted for less a day) the effect was like a blackout. Everything that I knew and understood about rebuilding my life, making myself whole, and being a good parent evaporated at the false prospect of my heart filling with love.

I made it eleven months.

I thought I had it licked. At about ten months another woman warned me, telling me I reminded her a lot of herself. She, too, had worked to stay sober so she could get her kids back. She relapsed several times before she was able to embrace the idea that she owed it to herself to become sober. I didn't understand the notion of becoming sober for myself. I believed that living together with my kids as a family again was the best gift I could give myself.

I started staying out all night with different men, each of whom said he loved me, of course. Soon I was using every time the girls went to stay with their father, and then when they were with me, leaving them alone all night.

I stole from them. I took the vacation money and bought cocaine. One morning near dawn, I sat, immobile, in a dope house while my daughters started their first day at a new school. I kept looking at the clock, wanting more than anything to get up and leave. I wanted to be with my girls. I couldn't move. When I finally made it home, they were gone. They had gone to school on their own and waited hours for me when they got home. Eventually they called their father who came and got them. It was probably just as well. I had brought home my latest man.

Are you getting tired of reading about my terrible mistakes? Are you beginning to think I am irredeemable? Holding these memories in my mind all at once so that I can tell my story, even after two decades of sobriety, fills me with a shame so deep that I am overcome with how *worthless* and *bad* I am. So I call my sponsor, discuss it with my therapist, and talk about it in meetings. I allow the dark murk of it all to flow to God who does not condemn me. I am worthy of being alive. God knows every detail of my past and still loves me.

Cleotha's daughter Kayla introduced me to her friends as her "white sister." She used cocaine, and we often got high together. Cleotha must have been aware of this, but she turned a blind eye. I fed my relationship addiction with Cleotha's son Gabe, maneuvering to become his true love in the first week after he came to live with her. He introduced me to crack, "ready rock" he called it, smoking being so much safer and more convenient than fooling around with needles. I had never smoked cigarettes and thought smoking crack wasn't for me. Gabe taught me how to inhale. I learned so well that a few years later, in the drug house, I would kindly teach the young girls how to inhale the crack they smoked so they could stand to get back out on the stroll to get $20 to buy another rock.

Gabe and I used to sing duets together, but never in public. Now I wonder if it wasn't because he didn't want to be seen so close to a white woman. He didn't have much sense about practical things. He almost bought a Cadillac that had blue smoke billowing from the tailpipe. I talked him into a gold 1974 Thunderbird, which he would often lend me so I could shop and do other errands. I loved driving around in that car.

Soon, I got pregnant with Gabe's baby. He was not happy. I'm sure he had feelings for me, but he was getting flak from his friends for being with a white woman. He even told me that before he met me, he always held the opinion that Black guys should not be with white women. He didn't want me to be seen driving his car anymore, and he certainly didn't want to have a baby with me. We had our first big fight over whether I should get an abortion. He shoved me against a wall, but I stood up to him.

"Don't you dare get violent with me!" I shouted. He backed off.

Even though I didn't think it was right, I scheduled an appointment with a doctor who did abortions. He was cold and unfriendly.

"How about a hysterectomy, too?" he asked. "We have a sale going on now—two for one!"

I was horrified, but set up the appointment. I prayed for Gabe to change his mind. The night before my abortion was to happen, I started bleeding. Having been through this before, I went to bed. Gabe, however, wanted to get high and sent me out to get some cocaine. Off I went.

The house where I bought drugs was on a hill, and while I was standing in the driveway, chatting with the dope man's girlfriend, the car started to roll backwards. I leaped through the open window of the moving car. Balanced on my stomach, half in and half out, I grabbed the steering wheel and guided the car safely down the hill. As I drove it back up the hill, my belly was cramping. I finished our transaction without getting out of the car. In the morning I woke up in a puddle of blood and cancelled the appointment with that awful doctor.

The next time we ran out of rock, we were broke. We did have a $150 money order all made out to pay our share of the light bill. It wasn't hard for Gabe to convince me to change it into a blank one so he could go cash it and get more rock. I waited for hours for his return, straining for the sound of the T-bird, watching the wall for the reflection of his headlights. By morning, he still wasn't home. It was hard to be angry when I was so worried he was hurt or in jail.

I went to Cleotha's house, and she didn't seem very concerned. Later that day he called me, from Seattle. He had intended to come home, he said, but something made him get on the freeway and drive all night. He was going to stay there and spend a little time with his dad. It was nothing personal, he told me, just one of those things that wasn't ever going to work out. He asked me to take all his stuff over to his mom's.

Once more, I was shocked and heartbroken. Cleotha was angry about the money but remained my friend. She moved me into a little house she owned nearby. She introduced me to people as her "girl," and impressed upon her friends that I was proof that not all white people are bad.

In that little house I became more and more addicted to crack cocaine, even though I managed just enough control not to use in front of the children when they came to visit. I waited until they were asleep. I had a couple of boyfriends, all of them Black, and the neighbors didn't like it. Every time I took my children outside to play or to get into the car to go somewhere, I felt stares and heard murmured comments. I woke up one day with someone's trash dumped on my porch. Another time I found a dead bird in my mailbox. When I confronted a neighbor who made a rude remark, an altercation ensued. Cleotha was sorry I was having trouble but said you can't do much when people are angry about a white woman having Black children and Black boyfriends.

Concerned about the safety of my children, I moved a few blocks away, into a small white house that had two bedrooms and a full basement. The number of men coming and going to buy and sell drugs, escalated. I would often smoke crack all day, chasing a repeat of the bliss of the morning's first high. When it was obvious that wasn't going to happen, I'd take my craving to a bar and drink to take the edge off the anxiety. The chance of meeting a man there who had some rock was always pretty good. I'd bring him home and start the cycle again.

I was miserable. I asked God to help me stop, but nothing happened. The pull of the drug house was so much stronger than any belief that I might get my children back. The misery of losing my children just made me want to get high that much more. I hatched a plan for ending this life I hated when I couldn't possibly stand to be myself one more day.

I chose my spot on the bridge in Riverfront Park one night when I had stumbled out of the bar and found myself there watching the smooth current flow under me. It was so hard to bear the ruin I had made of myself and my family. When I was unable to fight my overwhelming sense of worthlessness for another day, I would jump off that bridge and let the river carry me away to Spokane Falls, a journey I imagined as being graceful and painless. Having this plan, knowing there was an exit, allowed me to keep going for another few months.

Then came a night when I took stock of myself as I sat in the bar, desperate for cocaine, weary of how I had to debase myself to get it, ashamed of how many people I had let down. Everything about me was broken and wrong. I had failed at everything I tried. My parents had been right all along. I was *bad.* I was *worthless.* The time had come.

I guzzled a couple more drinks to maintain my courage and set out to end my life. My sense of purpose made me feel powerful as I walked through that park for the last time and stepped onto the bridge. I was climbing onto the railing, drunk out of my mind, looking forward to how the river would float me into oblivion, when I looked down. Beneath me was nothing but rocks. Rocks! It was August. The river was a just a trickle. There was no way I was going to hurl myself down on a pile of rocks!

I screamed. At God. I was so mad. He had stuck me in this stupid, horrible life, wouldn't help me with my problems, and now he'd even foiled my attempt to get out.

"What do you want from me???" I called Him every evil name I knew.

Jeremy couldn't leave those motorcycles alone. One night he and some buddies rolled a motorcycle down some stairs and through a church door. Another time he threw a rock through a showroom window because he wanted the motorcycle that was inside. He grew taller and ever more handsome with those heavy blonde lashes and golden eyes. Girls couldn't get enough of him. Jeremy reveled in the flash that put him at the center of attention. He never went anywhere without an entourage.

One day while riding the bus I overheard a group of teenage girls gushing about that "white guy that acts Black." Jeremy for sure. In his elementary school years, we lived in apartments where all the other families, and thus all his playmates, were Black. Phil and Derek were his father figures and he looked up to them and imitated them in every way. He was starting to get involved with gangs. It wasn't that he acted and talked "Black." He acted and talked like the people he knew and admired. He looked unusual, but in every other way, he fit in.

The girls on the bus were excited about the parties that Jeremy threw every Thursday night. One of them had been with him the Thursday before and another was excited about what might happen the coming Thursday, the day after tomorrow.

"Hey!" I almost called to them, "That's my son you're talking about!"

But I didn't. I was just some white lady at least as old as their mothers. They weren't interested in Jeremy's mom. I stared at my hands and listened, trying to decide if I was proud.

When Jeremy went to prison, I wrote him letters and put money on his books, hoping that might bring us closer when he got out. Prison was hard for him. They called him a wigger—that's "W" for "white," and you can figure out the rest. The white guys thought he was weird because he moved and talked like a Black man. The Black guys thought he was some kind of informer. He went in for stealing motorcycles. When he got out, he started dealing drugs and guns.

When I first started using, I used to say that I admired the girls that worked the streets, but that I didn't have the heart or the courage to do that. Then one night as I left my favorite dope house, craving more but out of money, a car stopped to offer me a ride. I got in. The guy told me that if I gave him a blow job, he would give me $20. Twenty minutes later I was back at the dope house buying another rock. So easy, so quick, and so meaningless. At least that's what I told myself. The need for the pain relief and the fear of being without it was stronger than any inclination to notice how I was debasing myself.

Once I found out how easy it was to get $20 for a rock, I quickly became a 24/7 addict. Sometimes the rock was good, sometimes not. Sometimes the guys were easy, sometimes they were mean. Sometimes the dealers were meaner. Sometimes I had to do the dealers as well as the dates on the streets. Sometimes the dealers took my money and never came back. That was just how things went in my new way of life.

I was with a guy who was taking too long. He was a lot drunker than I had realized at first, or else I never would have taken him back to where I was living, a trailer over by Broadway and Park. Drunks were annoying because they always took longer. At the end of his time and then some, I let him know he needed to finish up. He still refused to stop. I could tell he would never get where he was trying to go. Finally I said I was sorry, but we were done. He was mad, but he left.

I had twenty dollars I needed for a rock. Before I could leave to go find it, my locked door smashed open and ricocheted across the room. He was back. He beat me up—face? kidneys? gut? There's no way to sort this one from all the others. When he quit, he pried the twenty-dollar bill out of my clenched fist.

Losing the money was the worst. I'd have to go back out there and do some other guy for the twenty I needed to halt the screaming inside me. I lay there beat-up on the floor. Maybe I could stand up, but no way I could get back out on the stroll. My life had become one big ocean of highs and the debasement it took to get high. It held neither hope nor promise.

Maybe you think that this was going to be my moment of change. Maybe you think that finally, understanding the consequences, I would show a litte willpower, "get some help," and "straighten my life around." Or maybe, like me, you've "been there."

I grabbed a bottle of amitriptyline I was taking for depression. It had just been refilled. I washed them all down with the beer I had left.

The guy I was seeing came home and saw the empty pill bottle lying on the floor beside me where I sat like a zombie, still drinking, obviously beat-up. He locked me in and ran to the Zip Trip on the corner to call 911. I climbed out the bedroom window and ran away from the direction where I saw the lights of the ambulance coming. On Broadway, I flagged down a vehicle and got in. I don't remember anything after that.

It was a grade-school boy cutting through the park who found me, I was told. He ran home to his mother and cried that there was a dead lady with no shirt on lying in the bushes. She called 911, hurried to the park, and started CPR.

Meanwhile I was in hell. Encased in black tar where I could neither move nor scream for help. Trapped, I was more alone than I had ever been in my life. This was a place of complete nothingness. No sound. No light. No one. Not even God. Only me and my awareness of how *worthless* I was. I had never felt this kind of terrorizing loneliness.

I cried out for God. Not because we had been on very good terms lately. Not because I believed that God gave a shit anymore about what happened to me.

Suddenly He was there. In that awful, devastating place. Even though I called Him a motherfucker and blamed Him for not saving me from myself, He was still willing to envelop me in His love and carry me away from that place.

When I came to, I had no idea where I was. I had no idea who I was. A male nurse approached me. He wasn't God. Terrified that I was about to be sent back into the black tar, I raised a foot, delivered a kick right into his chest and sent him flying. I saw him hit the wall and slide down, then I was out again. When I woke, I was tied to the bed. I was conscious of my body and grateful I had one. God had raised me from the dead.

When I got out of the hospital this time, I was more determined than ever to stay sober. Suicide was never going to be an option for me again. The horrible realm of black tar was worse than the life I was trapped in. I moved into a house with many bedrooms in the Hillyard neighborhood in Spokane. The other tenants, all of them male, were sober and supporting each other in trying to stay clean.

At first they were sober, anyway. One by one they relapsed, and the ugly in them emerged. Alcohol ramped up the misogyny. One crowed about whiskey being "liquid balls." They yelled at me for no other reason than that "women were all alike." One guy had a dog named Butthead who ran away. Somehow, this became my fault. He cornered me in the kitchen.

Another roommate arrived, drunk. He waved a hammer and offered to bash my head in. I managed to make it to my room and call the police while they banged on the door.

Homeless again. But I stayed sober. For a time.

I didn't always have to "ho" myself on the stroll to get money for crack, because I had a talent for writing bad checks. With my charm and gift of gab I could make any clerk think I was trustworthy. When I bought groceries—sometimes with a list from the dope man—I would write a check to get the maximum cash over the purchase amount and convince them to trust me when it turned out I had "forgotten" my ID. I would write the same phony driver's license number on every check, so I never seemed confused about what the number should be. I accounted for my bedraggled appearance with a concocted story about renovating a house, which made me seem capable and strong. Then I'd walk out with hundreds of dollars' worth of groceries and cash.

I acquired a reputation for being good at this. If someone furnished the checks, I turned them into money. They gave me a rock and some of the cash for my trouble.

I victimized just about every grocery store in the Spokane area, large or small. Jack-in-the Box, McDonald's, Zip's—any place that would take a check was an opportunity. I remember once pulling up to the window at a downtown Arby's to pay for a very large order and the clerk yelled, "You owe us lots of money!" We hit the gas and drove away laughing. "Guess we better not come back here!"

I had a value system. Or at least I did, once. My addictions took precedence. I was selling my body and writing checks that took money away from other people. The thrill of the check writing itself became its own kind of addiction. Since I've been clean, I have never allowed myself another checking account. Not because I wouldn't have been able to con another bank into giving me one.

With crack cocaine you didn't need sleep. Or food either, for that matter. As long as I had alcohol, I could stay awake for up to two weeks at a time. A good hit immobilized me, which was fine, because it also put me into a state of utter bliss. When the high wore off, I jump-started myself with a beer and spent the rest of the day and night chasing a high as good as that first one.

The hours between 3AM and dawn were the hardest. That's when the dealers slept and even an addict knows better than to wake a dealer up. The bars were closed. I would ride around with random collections of people, other addicts looking for drugs. We picked up other people if they said they might know where to find some. Usually we did, but if we turned up empty, I could drink enough to go home and sleep for a bit and restart the search as soon as I woke up.

That's how I found myself walking around one morning before dawn, intending to get some beer and see what else I could find. I had money. I didn't need to get into the car that stopped and asked if I "needed a ride." But I did. The guy was big—dark hair, olive skin, good looking. We parked in the lot of a school close to the house where I had been partying all night. I hoped no one would see us.

He gave me the money and climbed on top of me. After a few minutes I heard voices approaching and told him he needed to hurry. He spat that he "wasn't hurrying nothin'," which made me realize I had one of those guys who wanted to make it last as long as possible. That might be great in a relationship, but rough for business. I told him eagerly not to hold out on me and pretended to climax. Sometimes that helped. Not this time. We couldn't go on, I told him. Not in a school parking where it was starting to get light and someone, maybe a family, could walk by at any moment.

Furious, he jumped back into the driver's seat and said we would just go somewhere else. I refused. He had taken up enough of my time, so it was his own fault if he couldn't finish. I started to get out of the car, but he grabbed me and pulled me back. He was drunk, but he was strong. He reached in my pocket where he had seen me put my little money purse and clawed to get his money back. I couldn't break free. He stepped on the gas and sped away.

"Where are you taking me?" I demanded.

"To the river."

This was in the days when there was a serial killer preying upon Spokane prostitutes. We all knew never to let anyone take us anywhere further than a couple of blocks from the stroll. When he pulled onto the freeway, I rolled down the window, leaned out, and started pounding on top of the car, all the while trying to memorize this guy's face. I took in the freckled shoulder, the marijuana leaf tattooed on his right arm. It was a yellow 80s Mustang. I noted the grip on the shifter, the neatly folded laundry in the back seat, everything I could tell the police if I lived to do so.

He drove with one hand and pounded me with the other. I kept banging on the top of the car. A blue van pulled up alongside us and started to honk. I reached for the key in the ignition. There was no way I was going to go to that river. He slammed my arm down. The van stuck with us when he pulled off the freeway and turned into an abandoned drive-in movie theater where I used to go with my family.

I managed to unlatch the door and braced it open with my foot. He squealed around in a circle and shoved me out. I could see the pavement speeding beneath me as I sailed away from the car in a sitting position. I heard my angel choir.

"Keep your head up..."

I skidded across the gravel, my chin tucked against my chest until I couldn't hold it there anymore and my head slammed down, hard. I was conscious of people running towards me and people hollering from their yards. Then I remembered it was Memorial Day, noticed how beautiful and warm it was, could smell barbecue. As the Mustang sped away, I saw a red rag like the ones mechanics use, sticking out the back, above the license plate, hiding the number.

I was swallowing the blood that flowed from my nose and lips. I knew from all the beatings I had taken over the years that I would look like hell the next day if I didn't get ice on my face right away to stop the swelling. I heard sirens and shouting. Concerned faces peered down at me.

"I'm so sorry," I said. "I need ice."

The ambulance came. As they lifted me onto the gurney, I thought, *I'm not in the river.*

According to Mama, the children heard all about it on the TV news. Because every time there was a news story about a woman found unconscious or dead, they gathered around the TV to see if it was me. *What kind of a mother is that?* she asked.

I healed up, but nothing changed. On the stroll I was known as the ho who sang hymns. The route: ho enough for rock, get high in one drug house or another, swear to quit, come down, go to a meeting, get back out on the stroll to earn another $20 for a rock. Maybe find it by drinking in a bar for a while.

Walking down the stroll one day, looking for someone to pick me up, not desperate yet, but knowing I was going to need another $20 soon to buy a rock, a car approached. I smiled and waved in my usual flirty style. Jeremy was behind the wheel.

"Whore!" he yelled, and screeched away.

A police car took off after him, sirens blaring. I listened to the chase. It sounded like the sirens had stopped at the 7-11 on the other side of the highway. I prayed for my son who hated me. About 15 minutes later, I heard another approaching vehicle and once again turned around with my ready smile. The lights of a police car went on. Busted. Jeremy got the police to let him go by ratting me out.

In a room at the police station, a detective pulled out a stack of different people's checks, all in the same handwriting, all with the same driver's license number written on them. He went through them with me, one check at a time, asking what I had used the money for. The ones that had bought groceries for my children were set aside. Each one that I had used for drugs and partying represented a felony I would be charged with. I thought that was pretty decent of him.

In jail I was put on the medical floor, segregated from the rest of the women, because I was diabetic. I was in a cell by myself with my own bathroom, shower, and TV. Other than the guards, who were friendly enough, there was no company. I read a lot of books and got all the cocaine out of my system. This was a good thing. But it wasn't enough to keep me from relapsing almost as soon as I was released.

Cleotha had a special room at her house all made up for me when I got out of jail. As always, it felt like home there. She understood me. Her family made me feel welcome. She knew for me the key was in the music, that singing brought me into the presence of God. The room was small, but cozy, and there was a window right at eye level by the bed. I stayed awake at night staring at the stars, reaching out for God.

Then I relapsed. Again.

I met a guy looking for drugs one night. We hit it off so well that he moved right in with me. My kids called him Daddy. We were married a few weeks later at the Hitching Post in Coeur d'Alene, a place where everyone went to get married in a hurry. I thanked my friend Sandy for introducing us by giving her a carton of cigarettes. I'm sure I wrote a bad check for them.

For our honeymoon, we stayed in Sandy's apartment while she stayed at my house with the kids. We argued and smoked crack until dawn when we ran out of money. So we woke up Sandy to try to get money from her. A disaster of a wedding. And a disaster of a marriage.

Soon I was pregnant. I thought that with a baby to love, our marriage would calm down. He didn't react when I told him. Unwittingly, I'd chosen a moment when he was watching a cop car down the block, concerned that the cop was waiting for him to get in his vehicle and drive away with his suspended driver's license. He'd been drinking all day and started throwing furniture around, roaring like a crazed animal. Neighbors called the police. We told them it was just an argument. We got off with a lecture and a strong warning. On Cleotha's advice, I started dropping a little Benadryl in his beer if he was getting too drunk. It made him fall asleep.

My new husband and I made a pact not to smoke any more crack because of the baby, but I caught him in the garage, smoking a hit. If he wasn't going to keep his promise, I didn't have to keep mine either. I went to Sandy's house. She told me she had used when she was pregnant with several of her kids, with no ill effects. She reminded me that it wasn't good for the baby if I was stressed out all the time. She helped me find some. I began poisoning my unborn child.

After about two months of using, even I knew it wasn't right to do this to my baby. I checked myself into the treatment center at Deaconess Hospital. Right away, the staff started talking to me about abortion. It was still early enough in my pregnancy. They recommended I have one, lest I had a baby who was not okay. Abortion, to me was murder. Every baby was a gift from God and the love I always shared with a newborn kept me from despair.

My pastor came to see me. He recommended the abortion. My younger children's foster mother came to see me. She had a daughter that was harmed by drug use during pregnancy. She reminded me how hard it was to take care of her, with her many difficulties. I was the one who had gotten pregnant and believed the baby was entrusted to my care. If the baby was affected by my drug use, I would still love and care for it. To kill the baby because of mistakes I had made felt completely wrong to me.

Janet Baxter chimed in. She assured me that I would not get my kids back if I remained pregnant. I agreed to the abortion.

I thought it would be a simple procedure, not so bad as a miscarriage. I was wrong. It happened in two stages. First, I had to go in and have an implant that dilated my cervix and made it possible for the doctor to remove the baby the next day. It would also kill the baby, which would make the removal easier. So for twenty-four hours my baby suffered. During that time I felt it kick for the first time. Then it died.

The procedure the next day was just like the D&Cs I had with my miscarriages. I cried through the entire thing. The doctor was concerned, asked if I was in pain. I told him no, I was crying because I didn't want this abortion but had to do it to get my kids back. After he completed the procedure, he came around to the head of the table, held me, and told me how sorry he was. I sobbed in his arms for a long time. He didn't hurry me or tell me I had done the right thing. I am so grateful for his compassion. This was the worst thing I had ever done in my whole life. I had demonstrated that I was unable to live by my own convictions. I was *bad.*

When I went back to treatment, which is to say, went from the third floor of the hospital back to the fourth, I called Janet Baxter and told her what I had done.

"Good work," she replied.

Next time we were in court, she told the judge that I had not completed my treatment successfully because I had left the facility two days in a row. Nobody told me that could happen. I had been tricked into murdering my unborn child.

Once again, I lost everything I cared about. But I hung on to my sobriety.

I decided to open my own recovery center, even though everyone I respected in recovery told me I wasn't ready and should wait. I did not know how to wait. The need in the community was so great. I was inspired by the sponsor I had at the time, Sister Teresa. I watched her start the Women's Drop-in Center where I attended meetings every day. My center would complement her center by accepting anyone and offering services 24 hours a day.

A site opened up that was down the street from the courthouse and kitty-corner from the city's largest homeless center. The shelter staff agreed that my center would be a great help to their residents and would fit in with the food bank and resources for financial, housing, and other assistance that that could be found in the neighborhood. Finally, God was opening every door, pushing me to help my community with my experience and newfound hope.

The center was decorated by people from the neighborhood. They made artistic window displays and put out a sidewalk board. A reporter from a local TV station came with a photographer to do a story on us. Soon all kinds of donations came in from area churches as well as private citizens.

In addition to 24-hour meetings and support, we had an exchange program for household items. People brought in unneeded goods—dishes, cookware, small appliances, clothing, food—and could take away what they needed. The children also had their own exchange program where they could bring toys they had outgrown and swap them for something different.

I lived in the center. Anyone could wake me up to talk or listen when they needed company during the long and often tempting nighttime hours when the craving told them to seek out a crack dealer to ease their pain. During the day, meetings were held in a room with a big window where mothers could keep an eye on their children in the playroom while telling their stories and encouraging each other.

Things were going so well that the church across the alley whose congregation had given us a lot of support invited me to speak at an event about addiction and recovery. Sister Theresa called me up to the podium after a young nun finished speaking about how "we" had a responsibility to help "them," the addicts and drug dealers who worked the opposite side of the street.

As I took the mic to speak, facing the block where I used to buy drugs, a young man I knew from my using days walked past and called out, "Hey, Trish!" I greeted him by name in return. Then I told my audience that I was part of the "us" as well as part of the "them." We just weren't all that different. They hung on my every word. I felt I had really made Sister Theresa proud. Later, she told me that on that day, she feared I was headed for a relapse.

One of the most dangerous things that can happen to someone newly recovering from addiction is to have too much too good too fast. They become high on their success, which isn't really success. It's just another high. All-consuming activity takes the place of the all-consuming desire for the drug. At the first difficulty, not yet having engaged in the hard work of changing their life, they'll revert to the old, familiar behavior.

I don't remember how the beer got brought into the center. I don't remember popping open my first can. What I do remember is that by the end of the night I was smoking cocaine. In my center. The dream I had built from scratch was ruined by the time I'd taken that first sip of beer. The center was gone within 24 hours. And I was back at it again in full force, taking up my 24/7 crack habit right where I had left off when I quit 11 months earlier.

I can now look back and see the mistakes I made. I had not put my program first. For a long time, I put my children first, getting clean for them instead of looking deeper into myself for what I needed to learn. This time I put every addict in Spokane first. I did not take the suggestions made by the people I had trusted to guide me. It was like going to a doctor for a deadly condition and throwing away the medicine on the way home. I was not the first person in the world to do this.

Amazingly, Cleotha continued to let me stay with her. I got sober again, returned to meetings. Twice I had made it to eleven months. At that time, in 12-step programs, a person who had a full year of sobriety was thought to be through the worst of it. They might begin sponsoring other people. People didn't expect them to relapse. Today, it takes more like five years of sobriety for a person to gain enough experience and credibility to be considered ready to sponsor someone else. Anyone who has gone to meetings for very long knows someone who looks forward to reaching a sobriety milestone only to relapse just before they get there.

I resolved not to do that again, kept going to meetings, and was determined to stay sober again.

Cleotha had another tenant, Jayson, who seduced me—sort of. It only took minutes for me to be in love. He told me that a single hit would get the cravings out of my system and restore me. He brought me a rock, and of course I smoked it. I was immediately sneaking back out on the ho stroll, making money, buying my "very last" rock, smoking it, and going back out for more. The guilt and shame mounted with each trip but weren't enough to stop me.

Soon I was pregnant. Jayson was delighted. It would have enhanced our relationship, except for the troublesome fact that I was using. Not just occasionally, but every day. It was the only way I could escape the shame of my failures, all of them proof that I was weak and irredeemable.

Jayson and I had a row which carried down to Cleotha, who wanted to know what was going on. "She's drunk," Jayson called out in disgust.

"You? You are *drunk?*" The fury and betrayal in her voice were impossible to deny. I got up, left the house, and never returned. Cleotha bagged my things and left them outside. I retrieved them after dark so she wouldn't see me. Cleotha is no longer alive. I wish I could thank her for believing in me as long as she did.

Crack had eroded my value system to the point that I saw prostituting myself as a way of being independent. To get a rock, I could stroll down East Sprague until someone offered me a "ride" and in less than an hour be making my way to the dope man, cash in hand. But it was safer and easier if you had a man. People who might mess with you knew who you belonged to. He would drop you off to ho and wait for you around the block with the car window open just a slit. When you came back with money, you slipped it through the window and set out again. When you'd brought back enough for both of you to get high, he'd say, "Get in!" and off you'd race to the dope man. That always meant you had to ho enough for his rock as well as yours. And you probably lived in a motel room that you paid for, too.

Jayson found us a motel room on Sprague Avenue. I would prostitute myself from there to the Hoot Owl at the other end of Sprague, attend a meeting and ho back home again. Nobody can live like that sober. I got tired of paying Jayson's motel rent while he never did anything besides sit in the car and wait for me to get him high. I found a little apartment in a converted garage. I dragged in a mattress and box spring from the yard and threw it down on the floor. Then I went for a walk around the neighborhood, ran into some using buddies and brought them home. This was my first step on the road to running one of the biggest and most successful dope houses in Spokane.

5. Drug House

Addicts who needed a place to get high were welcome in my garage flop if they behaved themselves and brought me some rock. I was still making money on the stroll, too, and soon had enough to move into a better place, a three-bedroom house two blocks from East Sprague.

In recent months there had been much outcry from the area's residents who wanted to do normal things like eat or shop along East Sprague. When their children walked those blocks on their way to and from school, they'd encounter girls on the stroll and addicts passed out on the street. They might be offered sex or drugs. When the police cracked down, the sex and drug trade moved to houses like mine in the very neighborhoods where the folks complaining about us lived.

Word got out. Girls came in off the stroll to use the shower, recover from a rough date, or get a little sleep. Maybe you picture them the way hookers are

153

portrayed in film—wearing heavy makeup, glittery hot pants, and platform heels. To imagine the prostitutes on the East Sprague stroll, picture instead torn cutoffs, acne, and cheap sneakers. I was in my early 40s. These girls were children.

I gave them toothbrushes. I had a lot of pink clothes—that being my favorite color at the time. I let the girls borrow them and soon, most of the girls on the stroll were wearing pink. People called them "Trish's girls."

They had the types of disputes that any sisters would have. They stole from each other, so I organized a system of milk crates where each one could store her belongings and I kept a watchful eye on them. Sometimes I protected them—from dealers and from each other. I wouldn't allow anyone to use violence in my house to settle a dispute. When the no-violence rule was tested, I put a quick end to the fight, often at my own injury, lest they mistake kindness for weakness.

I was a mother. I was a pimp. I was a dope dealer. I was a friend. Each one of those girls earned a special place in my heart. And they knew it, even if they couldn't admit it.

Everyone came there—gangsters, dealers, and people who used. The dope men could leave a satchel with me and count on returning later with the amount of money agreed upon. Anyone who bought at my house had to give me a little, as did anyone who smoked there. I didn't have to go out on the stroll to support my habit.

Guys often became a problem when their money and dope were gone. They got tweaky and paranoid, jumping up at the slightest sound, peeking out the curtains every few minutes, ruining everybody else's high. I was strict. I made tweakers leave.

A sharp rapping at the front door would also ruin a high, so no one was allowed to walk up and knock. The rule was for people to tap at the side window and then come around the alley to the back door, jiggle the handle, and walk in. There was traffic every hour of the day and night. I was the CEO of that place. The whole thing worked. Too bad I was also steadily poisoning my unborn child.

We learn as children not to get in cars with strangers, but any woman working the streets does exactly that multiple times a day. In Spokane at that time, one of those strangers in a car was having sex with prostitutes and then shooting them in either the head or the heart. He buried their bodies or dumped them, usually along the river somewhere. I had seen the vehicle they were looking for. I believe I rode in the car with him once, but I made him laugh and he let me go.

How many girls did he kill? At least eleven. That's how many bodies were found, but who looks for missing prostitutes? Many of them are runaways with fake names, trying not to be found. When a girl disappears, she could have left town with a man or spontaneously gotten on a bus to somewhere new.

I knew most of the victims. I was the last person to see Shannon alive. I remember a pair of sisters, not the names, but their stories. One of them had just had a baby. They were always fighting and worried about each other at the same time. In addition to the sisters there was Melody, the one that he buried in his yard beneath the window of the bedroom where he slept with his wife. Melody was so sweet and pretty. She and I used to work together, promising to look for each other later each time one of us got picked up. Barefoot Linda was always kind to me. The other girls admired her because she was so smart. Katie was in her 20s, but she was a child. She would steal anything from anybody. She had a tattoo of a rose on her leg to remind her of her daughter Rose who was taken away because of her addictions. They found her floating in the river in Riverfront Park. The police asked me to identify her body. I recognized the tattoo.

Jewel hid in a closet when her mom came looking for her, I told her I hadn't seen her daughter. She asked me to call either her or the police if I did see her.

"She comes here to be safe," I told her. "Would you rather she went to one of those other places where she'd have to perform sexual acts to get high? She won't get hurt here."

I looked that mother right in the eye and said that. I had a daughter the same age. I wondered how it would have felt to have someone say that to me. The guilt and shame multiplied. When Jewel disappeared but her body was never found, I hoped that maybe her mother showed up one day and whisked her away, even though I was sure that wasn't what had happened.

There was a dealer named Mike who came by regularly. He collected all the money the girls had and would come back later with a sack, which he gave to me to hand out. One time, however, Mike didn't come back for days. He didn't have the drugs and wanted more money. I waved a wad of bills at him.

"Where the hell do you think this comes from?" I shouted. Then I lectured him. "Don't you just wish you had the kind of courage that these girls do, going out on the stroll every night with that killer lurking around? They're scared to death about their own safety, worried about their friends, and still risk their lives to earn a just enough money to get something to make their pain go away. Then they bring that money to someone they hoped they could trust, and he takes off with it and doesn't come back."

Mike looked at the floor, faking remorse, waiting for the tongue-lashing to be over so I'd hand over the money. I told him to get out and never come back. There were plenty more guys where he came from. We didn't need someone who stole from us. The girls couldn't believe I had done that for them. Mike could get rough, so they knew I took a risk. We had to scramble to find some rock that night, but word had gotten out. Nobody ever walked off with our money like that again.

The dope house didn't exist in a vacuum. It was inside a wider circle of gangsters for whom the crack operation was just one among many illegal activities. Things worked better for them when prostitutes were safe, so anyone who broke the rules of my house or messed with my girls got a payback that kept all the others in line.

Jeremy was in that circle of gangsters by then, though I hardly saw him. He went back to prison for a while, but aside from him giving me a bag of crack before he turned himself in, we weren't in touch. We did trade off each other's reputations, however. I heard he introduced himself sometimes as "Trish's son." One night I was crossing the Monroe Street bridge and was confronted by a scary gangster-looking guy. I introduced myself as Jeremy's mom and could see the respect flood into his face. We leaned on the bridge railing and chatted like co-workers in the break room.

As long as the steady flow of drugs was arriving, I stayed awake for days. Sleep was risky after days of cocaine and booze because it came as complete unconsciousness, which is dangerous, even in your own house if your house is a place where no one can be trusted. I kept alcohol, cash, pipes, and lighters stashed under my pillow or tied around my neck. Even so, I would often wake up to find I'd been robbed of hundreds of dollars, money that was seldom my own, but owed to the dope man.

After one such theft, when the money was due to be paid to a guy known to be very dangerous, I awoke groggily, saw that the money was gone, screamed, and fell back to sleep. All the girls went out to get the money back, not by finding the culprit—that money was long spent. They put out the word about what had happened, went on the stroll, shoplifted, and begged anyone they could for loans. I awoke sometime later to find various amounts of money stuffed under my covers. Confused, I gathered up twenties, tens, and even smaller denominations just in time to pay a fearsome dope man who would have killed me if I didn't have it. I think he was as relieved as I was, and also surprised at how loyal my girls were. I never found out who had stolen the money. We had rock. It no longer mattered.

I must have been a spectacle as my pregnancy advanced, but I wanted for nothing. People brought me everything I needed for that baby. They set up a crib and a dresser filled with baby clothes. They rented a washer and dryer. I was ready to be a mother, but not ready to stop using. On the rare occasions when I was alone, and aware of myself, I cried and begged God to protect the baby from me.

Contractions started a few months early. This was familiar from the six children I'd already had, so I refused to see a doctor and just put myself to bed. I had more help and company than I ever did living with a man. People reminded me to take my prenatal vitamins, check my blood sugar, eat, and take my insulin.

Six weeks before the due date, I went into hard labor. One of the girls called 911, and an ambulance took me to the hospital where I gave birth to an eight-pound baby boy. Given my malnutrition and dehydration, his size was miraculous. Such a perfect boy! I held him often and sang to him. Then I returned him to the NICU where he had to stay until he was no longer addicted to cocaine.

Janet Baxter came to the hospital and told me I had exactly one chance to be able to take him home with me, a treatment center in the Tri-Cities. I refused and returned to my dope house, leaving my baby at the hospital alone to kick the poison I had given him. I took the bus to visit him a few times. Then I caught a cold and used that as an excuse for why I was no longer visiting. The truth is that the visits got in the way of my using.

My mother and Janet Baxter convinced me that if I went to treatment, I might be able to bring my baby home. I was packed and ready, but while I was waiting for the people who were going to pick me up and take me there, I got high "for the very last time" with one of the girls. I hid in the bathroom when she answered the door, told them I had gone out for just a minute and asked if they could come back a little later. They tried to get her to allow them to come in and look for me. They called my name. I hid behind that bathroom door, wanting to go with them so bad, but unable to move.

A few days later when I called to check on my baby, the nurse who answered told me he had gone home with his new parents.

I screamed, "You didn't have to take my baby!" Over and over, even after she hung up on me. What did I think was going to happen? Did I think really think I was going to raise that precious child in a dope house? No one came to my house that night. You can always find somewhere else to get high. I sat in the dark, alone, enraged at God.

I schooled everyone who came into the house about probable cause, lessons I remembered from law enforcement classes and PI work. No one was ever to open the door to my house for a cop. Cops can't see or smell anything through a closed door. They need a reason to go further and will be looking for one as soon as the door is opened and they can peer inside. They must tell everybody they're cops. The same isn't true for PI's or informants. They can pretend to be anyone and flatter you into chatting about things that were best kept to yourself. I told the girls to be especially careful with the taxi drivers, particularly when there was a "trainee" riding along.

There was a spot in the alley with an overhanging tree where a taxi could park hidden from sight. The girls called cabs for rides to and from my house. Drivers dropped dates off at the house sometimes, or they were sent to my house by dates to pick a girl up.

Many of the drivers were customers for sex, for drugs, or both. They did a lot of business with crack addicts on the hunt. Girls would just hop in and ask, "Where's the rock?" They rarely paid for rides with cash. Drivers knew a lot.

I seldom went out. The girls brought me beer. I could pay a hit in exchange for a trip to the store. I could always trust them with the money because they were addicts. When they brought my stuff home, they'd get a hit. Going shopping was so much easier than a stroll up Sprague. I gave them a rock for shoplifted clothes that I liked. It was complicated to leave. I'd have to trust one of them to watch over everything.

On one occasion, I did leave the house carrying several hundred dollars collected by a houseful of dope-hungry women. I knew where to find someone who would turn it into what we craved. When I climbed into the taxi waiting in the alley, the first thing out of the driver's mouth was, "Are you okay?"

"Why would you ask me that?" I asked.

"Well, you just came out of Trish's house. A lot of the people who come out of Trish's house are not okay."

"I'm all right," I snapped and gave him the address.

"I know that place." He nodded, and took off.

When we got to the destination, he asked, "You want me to wait at the store on the corner?"

"Yes."

"You must be on an errand," he suggested.

I didn't say a word. After I completed my errand, and returned to the cab, he asked. "Back to Trish's house?"

I nodded.

When we arrived, he said, "You be careful in there. And by the way—you never told me your name."

I waited until I was out on the pavement before I answered. "Trish," I said, and slammed the taxi door. That was the second-to-the-last time I left that house.

I reached a point where I hardly left my bed. I got high, came down, and smoked another rock. If I slept at all, I would reach for a beer from the stash behind my pillow the moment I awoke. The first thing I would want after the first drink was the first hit of cocaine. Usually that was not a problem because the reason I woke up in the first place was either that someone had arrived with drugs, or someone had arrived with money.

I was steadily losing weight, down to a size 2 from a size 16. If someone brought me a burger and a hit. I'd trade away the burger for another hit. I couldn't bear the sight of myself in the mirror. This is what my dying was going to be. I talked a lot about God. I sang. I wasn't going to kill myself. But that didn't mean I intended to live.

Cocaine made me vomit. Beer made me vomit. Sometimes I vomited blood. The girls were scared and knew they had to do something. They cleaned up the house, removed all the evidence, packed their things, called 911, and fled. The police officer who accompanied the paramedics gave me a choice—hospital or jail. They handcuffed me to the gurney.

In the ICU I was delusional. The girls were all out in the hallway, smoking crack and talking about me. They wouldn't come in because they didn't want to give me any. The nurses weren't feeding me enough. I was starving. Desperate for food, I snuck out of bed and rode the elevator down to the cafeteria. I would have to steal the food, since I had no money. It occurred to me that they wouldn't let me in barefoot, so I ducked into a break room, dug through the trash, and found two matching plastic bags to fit on my feet.

Dealing dope, writing bad checks and even prostitution had taught me that the way to blend in was to act as if I was supposed to be doing whatever I was doing. Confidently, I picked up a tray, loaded it with meats, cheeses, and a creamy chocolate desert with cherries. I sailed past the checkout ladies and back up to my room, exhausted but proud. I put the desert in the drawer of the bedside stand and decided to have a little rest before I dug into the rest. As I covered myself up, I heard a nurse's voice.

"Been on a little adventure, I hear." She said cheerfully. She took my beautiful tray of food. Somehow, she knew all the details of my crime. I waited for a while after she left before opening the drawer of my bedside stand. I ate that dessert in tiny, delicious bites.

When I left rehab that time, one thing was different, and it was the only thing that mattered. I finally understood that I had to learn to value my life the same way that God did. For all I had cursed Him and blamed Him, He was still the one who bailed me out of that tarry hell after my suicide attempt. My life mattered to Him. He wanted me to live. I had tried to get sober for my kids, for judges, for Janet Baxter, and to help other addicts. I had to learn what it meant to get sober for myself and then learn how to do it. If I didn't, I was going to die. If God thought my life was worth saving, then so would I. I was determined not to mess it up this time.

I was about to learn why willpower might get you sober, but willpower alone will not keep you sober.

6. Recovery

Three decades have passed since that day in Sacramento when I went to my first meeting, when I rocked in a chair, black-eyed and puffy-faced while Phil wailed, "Look what I've done!" You can't think straight when your head is swollen and your breath wheezes through a bloody broken nose. Your mouth can't make words when your puffy, bruised lips are as fat as hot dogs. I was confused by the way they talked to me as if I had a drinking problem, something I had never considered.

I never gave much thought to drinking. My parents, having both grown up in families rife with alcohol and violence, did not allow alcohol in the house. (Although this never dampened Mama's interest in the drunken fights between my aunts and uncles.) I usually drank pop or chocolate milk when Dawn and I cruised Riverside, though I did get drunk and have sex with a stranger on the eve of my wedding to Gordie. I started getting comfortable in bars with my PI work, so it was easy to socialize there. In bars, people bought me drinks. At the time, I would have said that alcohol was "just around," and sometimes I drank it. I only guzzled myself into a sloppy drunk as a strategy to prevent Phil from drinking. I went to the meeting to get a new strategy to stop Phil from drinking so we could fix our marriage and be happy.

The first step in a 12-step program is to recognize that you have a problem, an addiction, and you are powerless against it. I couldn't embrace that thought at my first meeting. People in 12-step programs talk about "working the steps," something you do with the help of a sponsor who has a lot of experience in the program. The 12 steps are principles which you use to examine your life as an addict as you figure out how to stay sober and move forward.

If you download the 12 steps and run through them like a checklist, they won't do you much good. Yes, I'm powerless against my addiction. Yes, my life is unmanageable. Yes, I have done terrible things and hurt people. Now I must make amends. Now I have a Higher Power and that relationship will save me. Now I'm back in the ring, riding in the relapse rodeo.

When you work a program, you take the steps one at a time, starting with the first one, and consider each one carefully. Your sponsor gives you exercises to do and is available to talk it all over with you, sometimes for hours, sometimes in the middle of the night. It takes weeks to work a step. As time passes, you understand more and more about the step and about yourself.

Even before I was ready to say I was powerless against an addiction, I understood that I had plenty of experience with being powerless. How powerless is a hungry baby crying alone in a dark room? Or a little girl whose only friend dies unexpectedly and nobody but playground bullies will talk about it? What about a tween girl whose angry father orders her to strip naked because she has no right to be wearing clean pajamas? Or when her husband makes her scrub the bloodstains from her miscarriage off the couch before she's allowed to go to bed? I was powerless in every physical fight I had with a man. When I was screaming "Eat carpet, bitch!" I was powerless against my own rage. I have never been more powerless than when I was in the tarry hell after I attempted suicide with beer and amitriptyline.

As all this came roiling up, the memories made me furious. At everybody. About everything.

It's that black hole. It has so much pain in it. Rage. Betrayal. Abandonment. Self-loathing. When you start stirring things around, you're powerless against what you might remember and how it feels to do so. That's why you have a sponsor you can call in the middle of the night when you want to relieve that wild, raw emotional pain with a fix of whatever your addiction is. It didn't take much to send me to the black bottom of that hole where I was *worthless* and *bad.* When that happened, my addiction told me I needed a hit, just one, to tide me over. So I called my sponsor. Again and again.

I was thirty years old at that first meeting. When girls that age, or even younger, walk into a center or come to a meeting for the first time, I feel such empathy for them. I call them "girls," even though I know they are women, because I am so tuned in to their vulnerability. I see the confused, hurting child that they cover with street-smarts and bravado. They are desperate and alone. They don't believe anyone can really know how terrible their experience has been. I can. Even if they don't believe me.

These days, one of the exercises I do first thing with a new sponsee is to ask them to write their name in the middle of a blank sheet of paper. Then in the space around their name, I ask them to write down their strengths and accomplishments until there's no room to fit any more on the page. Many of these girls are so broken and traumatized that they can't think of a single thing to put down. I was like that. The mere attempt made me feel as feeble as I did on the back porch with Daddy, knowing that anything I wrote would be laughable. If my sponsee can't fill the page on their own—and many can't—I have them go around to everyone they know and ask them to tell them three things they can write on it. They get their pages filled up.

Sometimes a girl sobs because it's terrible both to believe and not believe what's on that page. One minute she's crying about how ashamed she is to have had all these talents and opportunities and wasted them. The next minute she knows it's all a lie and what passes for strengths are accidents, or fake, and underneath is the real person who is worthless. An instant later she's consumed with fury at all the people who hurt or betrayed her on this ugly journey.

When that happens, I don't argue with her or criticize her logic. Because I've "been there," as they say. I know that thoughts like these have been devouring her from the inside for a long time. It's not my job to talk her out of anything. All I can do is be present through her agony, and gently remind her that those thoughts are ugly and wrong while she is beautiful and valuable.

When you work the steps, there is so much to observe and feel from just one sentence. For each person it's different. At the beginning, the answer to every question connects you with a different aspect of your anguish—rage, victimhood, shame, grief. It can send you spiraling away in any direction. A sponsor who has "been there" understands that the root of the problem has nothing to do with your being weak and lacking willpower. Together, you talk.

After my children were taken away and I was doing everything Janet Baxter said I had to do so I could get them back, I went to multiple meetings a day, seven days a week. I had a sponsor who listened to my spews of outrage and betrayal. She kept me hanging on long enough to get to my next meeting without reaching for the reliable pain relief of a hit of cocaine. I thought I was in pain because my children had been taken away. I railed against Gordie, my parents, and Janet Baxter because they had betrayed me and lied.

My fury was unmanageable. It would take a long time—decades—for me to realize how I'd been accumulating pain and rage since I was a bewildered baby, screaming alone, while her mother wished she would hurry up and die. When I tapped into those feelings, they would explode, welling up through me like lava in a volcano, filling me with an agony that one hit of cocaine would wipe away. That's how I relapsed. Again and again.

The last time I was in rehab, 21 years ago, after the girls in my drug house made the phone call that saved my life, I had a sponsor who listened to me for hours. I was so tired, so sick, and so sad. I would never get my children back. Some of them were already grown and none of them wanted to see me.

I blamed everyone, including God. When it occurred to me that what I was going through was the result of my own choices, that was more proof of how *worthless* I was. I'd fight to defend myself from that thought by saying that all my choices had been taken away from me by my family, by the system, by my disease, and by God. They were to blame for turning me into someone so *worthless*. They would never acknowledge how much pain they had caused. How I was I supposed to forgive them and heal?

My sponsor gave me an assignment. She told me to get out my notebook and write down 200 things I was grateful for.

"200?" I was astounded.

"Yep," she said. "200 things you are grateful for. And no repetitions."

I wrote down all the numbers until I got to 200. Then I started filling out the list. I kept it simple, only one or two words each. First, all the people I loved, starting with my seven children. Then, the people I loved but were mad at, the ones I blamed for everything. Then God, whose reliable presence had comforted me as a child. I wrote down the names of the angels who whispered and sang to me lest I abandon my own life. Already I had quite a few things on my list.

I had a roof above my head. I had not always had a roof above my head. I had food to eat. I had not always had food to eat, or due to cocaine, had been unable to eat. Then I started listing all the different foods that I had at my disposal. I also had insulin, and several other medications without which I would be very sick. Then each of my doctors. And everyone else who had ever helped me in a program. People from my neighborhood, from my church, and the church itself. My music, and all the songs and singers that I love.

There was my car, nothing fancy, but it got me from point A to point B. I had enough money to put gas in the tank. I considered all the places it took me— to meeting halls, to classes and groups. And all the people who had helped me there. As the pages filled up, my doom-and-gloom attitude lifted.

When got to number 200, I couldn't wait to show the list to my sponsor so she could tell me how well I had done. I was dismayed that she didn't want to see it. All those things were mine, not hers, she said. I wasn't to think I was doing the assignments to please her. I was doing them so I could realize that what I was writing was true. In other words, my recovery was for me, only me. Others might be glad about it but that wasn't the reason for it.

As I was closing my notebook, she gave me another assignment. 200 more.

"What?" I exclaimed. "That isn't possible."

"Yes, it is," she replied, lovingly. "It really is."

I began again. I listed phrases and slogans that kept me on track in recovery. Bible verses. I opened the refrigerator and wrote down everything I saw.

When I was a child, catsup used to come in glass bottles. There was a TV ad that played Carly Simon singing *Anticipation,* which described exactly my experience with those bottles as a youngster. I'd hold the bottle upside-down over my food, shake and pound, and when the catsup finally came out, it was in a huge red glop all over my dinner. Of course I had to eat it all, no way Daddy would let me scrape it off. Now, catsup comes in plastic squeeze bottles that are easy to aim so you squirt the perfect amount of catsup exactly where you want it, every time. Not only that, but you can also store them upside down, so you don't even have to shake them. I am grateful for plastic catsup bottles.

That feeling of gratitude can connect a person to their Higher Power.

"All this gratitude," I say to my sponsees, "Who are you grateful to?"

One of the things that confuses—or alienates—a person new to a 12-step program is the way everybody talks about their Higher Power. I thought I had that one nailed. Not only did I believe in God, but I could conjure the presence of God and angels at any time. God had sent me SnoBall and Angie Farrell, the kind aunt who gave me SnoFee, and my seven beautiful babies, but for the last years, no matter how much I prayed, He'd thrown nothing but pain and difficulty in my path. Our relationship was quite rocky, given all the screaming and cursing I sent His way. I didn't see why having Higher Power was going to make my life much better. Because for a long time, my Higher Power didn't have anything to do with God. For all those years, my "Higher Power" was the idea of getting my kids back. A perfect example of a Power that's not high enough.

When I use the word "God," girls roll their eyes. Some accuse me of ramming this "God-stuff" down their throats. I am a Christian. I study the Bible. But I didn't meet God in a church. I have had a relationship with God since I was a child. When I say "God" I am referring to a loving being for whom my life has value. Most of the girls haven't had this experience. Many have been abused by men who claimed their authority came from God. Others had prayed to God to help them in the past and felt He never answered.

Some girls are convinced that God is a fairy tale, and they aren't going to be taken in by all that stuff. Others look at the terrible things they've done and say they could never respect a God so foolish as to love them. Still others are so angry that God has allowed such awful things to happen to them—maybe even caused them—they can't see anything beyond the fury they direct His way.

I try to help the girls understand that it really doesn't matter how you picture your Higher Power, only that you can picture one. It doesn't matter what you call it, only that you realize you have one.

If it is a new boyfriend, the one who finally understands and truly loves you, that power won't be high enough. Nor the job or degree that will lead to your dream career if you just stay sober. Can it be the ocean, the universe, or the great chain of being? Perhaps. You work the steps. You find the words that make sense to you. You try to learn and understand what it means to give all the pain of your life to your Higher Power. Your Higher Power must be vast enough to absorb all that you are going to throw at it. Your Higher Power isn't going to pop into your life all at once, turning all the colors beautiful and fixing your pain. People who have been wounded and betrayed can't just open their hearts and find redemption. Understanding your Higher Power is a process.

The third step is the one where we embrace the fact that the way we have been managing things doesn't work. We work to discover our Higher Power and learn the role such a power takes in our recovery. That gives us a foundation to begin the inner inventories that come next. When we consider our misdeeds, the people we've hurt, and the ways we've lied to ourselves, everything we have been using drugs to forget comes back in full and terrible force. Unless we have a Higher Power to give all that anguish to, it will consume us.

Every time we are overcome by anxiety and hopelessness because of all the things we can't control, we can let them flow through us like a river and out to our Higher Power that will absorb them. Then we can center our attention on looking at ourselves objectively, sorting out and seeing clearly where we've been, who we were, and who we want to become. The steps teach us and help us to find out those answers.

When someone says they don't believe in God, I ask them who they are talking about when they say that? Is it possible to be so unique that you have no connection to the source of love and life of all the universe? I'm not trying to prove anybody right or wrong. I just want them to think about these things separate from their pain. When you feel alone and abandoned, you won't suddenly say, "Aha! I have been connected to something larger than me all along!" It takes a lot of consideration and self-examination to understand what that "something" could be and what that connection means for you.

It's important to work the steps in order. Lots of people, confused or put off by "all that Higher Power stuff" skip straight to Step 9, making amends. I did this. When you first admit to yourself that your actions as an addict have hurt people, the shame and guilt are extreme, as is the urge to be forgiven. You rush into the lives of those you've hurt, brimming with remorse, and begging their forgiveness. Because if they'll forgive you, maybe you aren't so *bad.* Chances are they've seen this before and don't believe you. If they do believe you, chances are you'll disappoint them, and they'll never believe you again. It takes a long time to be ready to ask for forgiveness. First you must work the steps until you can forgive yourself.

The women at the center that supported me every day were asked to help produce a program put on for women by women. It was to be at St. Joe's Auditorium, open to the public, and the entire Spokane community of women in recovery would attend. They asked me to sing the lead part. I was stunned. Of course I loved to sing and had been singing all my life, but I had no idea I was noticed. A dream was coming true. A picture of me appeared in the paper alongside an article describing the event.

I sang a Mariah Carey song called *Looking In*, about a woman who longed for change in her life. It was about me. It was about most of us. The whole program was such fun. In one of the numbers we line danced to "Achy, Breaky Heart." After every number we would collapse into each other's arms in giggles and squeals.

At the end there were cheers, applause and an exuberant round of bows and ovations. We hugged each other and laughed.

Then I saw my sister. What was she doing there? I had not talked to her since she was awarded custody of my three younger children. I was over a year sober by that time, but my sobriety had made no difference. She had not allowed me to have any contact at all. But there she was, parting the crowd, heading straight for me, beaming. She had seen the newspaper article. Behind her was my daughter. I almost didn't recognize her. She was becoming a woman. When she burst into my arms, all the cheering started up again.

I don't have much of a relationship with my sister today, nor do I communicate with that daughter. My sobriety doesn't seem to have impressed them nearly as much as all my misdeeds. They don't see me as someone worth knowing. Isn't this unfair? Don't I deserve compassion? Can't they see how I've been hurt? Why won't they recognize all the progress I have made these past decades? When these questions well up, bringing all their uncomfortable emotions, I can spiral my way into a full-blown pity party, retell my story with them at the center, the cause of my every misstep. My sponsor will help me talk my way through it.

The reality? How they picture me and why they think of me the way they do—all the things that torture me so—are completely out of my control. The rage and resentment that well up when I think about it are also out of my control. All I can do is open my heart and let all the devastation and regret flow to my Higher Power, to God. God can take it. Then what I have left is the memory of the love that shone from their radiant faces that day.

As my recovery progressed, the time eventually came for me to examine my relationship with Mama. Her words and deeds traumatized me from the very beginning of my life. As a child, I craved her approval and companionship. After she sided with Gordie and took him in when we separated, she was the obvious target for my rage and resentment. I used to call her up in the middle of the night, drunk and tearful, demanding to know why she had been so cruel to me.

As you work the steps with your sponsor, you have many chances to re-examine relationships that have gone wrong and recognize how nothing in the tangle of dysfunction is black and white. You try to imagine what it was like to be that other person. Stories about how Mama had hurt me poured out, each memory more painful than the next, until finally I began remembering some of the stories I'd heard about her childhood.

She listened to her parents chase each other with kitchen knives at night, wondering if only one of them would be alive in the morning. She spent long stretches of time living with her grandmother to escape the violence. Her father got her best friend pregnant when they were teens. She told me a story of how her bunnies in the back yard were her dearest friends. She cuddled them and they soothed her pain—until the day her father made her butcher them and cook them for her brothers. I don't remember her and Daddy ever enjoying each other's company. Did he use to slap her upside the head before he had us kids to beat on?

I had been sober for a decade when she became terminally ill. Daddy had died a year earlier. My siblings settled her into a nursing home without consulting me. I went to visit her and found her, head down on a table in the big dining room, crying and alone. She had always extracted promises from us that we would never put her in a nursing home, and there she was. I sprang into action and made good on my promise.

Soon, my mother was safe in her own house, with a hospital bed, and caregivers that came daily to change linens, help her shower, and see that she took her medications properly. I checked in often to make sure she was getting good care. We talked and mended our relationship.

I thought that if we could discuss what was painful about both her childhood and mine we would reach and understanding of how so much cruelty came my way and I could forgive her. But the topic was off limits. "Makes me too sad," she would say.

In recovery, forgiveness is tricky and layered. My sponsor told me to make a list of everything Mama didn't know. Not knowing doesn't excuse her behavior, but it explains it. She wasn't cruel because I was *bad.* My sponsor and I talked about how I was trying not to use the phrase "should have known better" to tear myself down. Was it fair for me to use the phrase to tear Mama down? My sponsor had me make lists of what I could and could not control in our relationship. I had control over whether I saw her at all. When I did see her, I had control over whether I was kind to her. Of all the regrets that I have in my relationship with Mama, I will never regret being kind to her at the end of her life.

I've forgiven Daddy, too. It's been a long, complicated process. We never spent any time together when we spoke with honesty and compassion. In painful bewilderment, I have asked so many times, "How could he do such things to me?" Eventually I began to genuinely wonder what must have happened to a person to turn them into someone who can pick a fight with their children by insisting that bald eagles are bald. It occurred to me that his idea that some people are so unfit for everything that they should never try anything is just as absurd as bald eagles having no feathers on their heads. The love, recognition and understanding that I so longed for him to give me were things he had never received, things he could not give himself, much less someone else.

My experience of him was terrible and unfortunate. It wasn't my fault that he hurt me. I deserved apologies, but whether I received them or not was out of my control. As I found ways to give all I couldn't control to God, I could accept that he lacked the tools to overcome his upbringing and be a good parent. He didn't do that on purpose.

I'm not close to either of my siblings. I never found enough common ground with my sister to form a relationship. My brother calls me occasionally when there is news in the family he thinks I should know about. So I was curious one spring day when I answered the phone and heard his voice. I leaned against the kitchen counter in my house in a small town an hour or so south of Spokane, wondering which aunt, uncle, or cousin had met with misfortune.

"Have you heard yet?" he asked me?

"Heard what?"

"I would have driven down to tell you in person, but I was afraid you'd find out before I got there."

"Find out what?"

"Jeremy was shot and killed by the police. It's on all the channels."

I heard screaming, loud, sustained screaming, and did not even realize that the sound was coming from me. My roommate came to the kitchen, found me on the floor and picked up the phone receiver. My brother was still on the line. The rest of that day unfolded somehow.

Jeremy was due to turn himself in the next day. This would be his third strike. He was looking at life. He had already signed papers giving custody of his two-year-old daughter to his girlfriend Suzanne. He threw himself a going-away barbecue. Every gangster, pimp, and dealer that served the Spokane area was there, along with their girlfriends and families.

He and Suzanne were both drinking hard. She was pushing his buttons and mocking him. Was she having a little fun? Showing off how she could get under his skin? Was the reality setting in that she was about to be left alone to parent someone else's toddler? People warned her to be careful. Jeremy was on his way to a blackout and well-known for beating up the women who loved him.

Suzanne brandished her pink knife, full of bravado. She was so proud of that knife.

"He tries to lay a hand on me, I'll stick him!"

How many times have I told girls never to carry a weapon unless they wanted to be killed with it? They would come into the house, scared of some dope man or pimp, and say they needed a knife for protection. It made me furious to watch them jeopardize themselves like that. I'd lecture. Any man can overpower you if he wants to. If you're fighting over a weapon, the fight will end when he uses it on you. Suzanne wasn't the first girl I knew who died that way.

They found Suzanne's pink knife in the house, covered in blood. Jeremy had a knife wound on the palm of his hand. Suzanne had stab wounds over her entire body. There was blood in every room of that house—on the walls, the floor, the furniture, the crib. On the baby. Oh, that girl must have fought.

Jeremy rolled her hemorrhaging body up in a blanket and laid her on the bed next to an open window where the neighbors could see, which they eventually did, and called the police. By then, Jeremy had gathered up his little girl, driven to his attorney's office, and said he wanted to change the paperwork so his sister would have custody of his daughter. He left the child there, called his sister, told her where his daughter was, and said he was going to kill himself.

He returned to the house where a police barricade was already set up. All the news outlets were there with vans and cameras. Jeremy hit the gas, slammed into the barricade, hopped out of the truck, and aimed a toy gun modified to look real at an officer.

There would be an investigation. It would reveal how many bullets had hit my son, the order in which they had struck him, and which one had killed him. So many official words that said he was dead before he hit the ground. He was thirty-seven.

If I hadn't been sober, I'd have been dead before nightfall, overdosing on everything I could get my hands on in hopes of stopping the pain. I am deeply grateful to my sober friends, the meetings I attended, and everyone in my circle who stayed by my side, while the eviscerating horror of Jeremy's death flowed through me, relentlessly, day and night. I gave it all to my Higher Power, to God. All of it. When I let it flow out of me, more welled up. I looked to Jesus for the strength to bear the suffering with dignity. If I had kept all that anguish inside, it would have consumed me. I would have found a way to die.

Everyone from the barbecue came to his memorial service and many others as well. I didn't know most of Jeremy's friends, but they were very kind to me. Gordie was there, looking as if he'd been torn apart. The pain of it was probably the first thing we'd agreed upon since the divorce. We treated each other gently.

Before the memorial service I tracked down every photo of Jeremy that I could find and made a poster of his whole life. We set it up on the table with his ashes. There on display was that beautiful boy I knew, so funny and smart. His sweet unspoiled face reminded me of how he woke up every day, eager to get out into the world to see what was going to happen next, always thinking three steps ahead of the people around him.

Jeremy had a reputation for being generous and polite. Jeremy also hurt a lot of people. Imagine who

Jeremy could have been if I hadn't been his mother. I was responsible for this.

Jeremy's death sent me right to the edge of the black hole. Everything that I tried not to think about myself was true. I was a terrible mother. He followed in my footsteps. My parents were right. I was *bad.* God gave me a beautiful son to love. I destroyed him.

I credit my sponsor and others in meetings who, by listening to me, kept me alive. I had forgiven my mother for the mistakes she made and accepted the fact that I was responsible for how I responded to those mistakes. It was—and still is—hard for me to use the same logic and forgive myself for what happened to Jeremy. People who cared about me gently reminded me, again and again, that Jeremy, a grown man, was responsible for his own choices. Without their support, I would have spiraled into believing that I was too *worthless* to live.

I think of him every day.

My recovery is my full-time job and number one hobby. Wherever I have lived I have found groups, meetings and centers I can be a part of. I'm not fooled by all these years of sobriety. I am still powerless against my addiction. I have no control over what might rocket me back to the place where only a hit of crack can relieve the pain. If there isn't a group or a center in a place I am living, I'll start one.

I became connected to a center that truly felt like home. Many of the young women were struggling with opioid addiction and all the terrible things that can go along with it—the abusive relationships centered on getting high, the neglected children, what you are willing to sell or trade for your next hit. I volunteered at the reception desk and greeted people. I could feel the waves of pain rolling off some of them as they came through the door. Few had very much clean time and most of them were very young. There was so much need there.

Beth broke a lot of hearts. She certainly broke mine. I wonder how many people felt the same way about me. Every passing thought of her makes me ask myself what I could have done differently, starting from the the first day she walked in.

A newcomer is always the most important person in a meeting. Everyone in the room knows how much courage it took for them to walk through that door, and how much fear and hopelessness walked in with them. Newcomers make us remember what it felt like when we were the newcomer, overwhelmed by the mess of our lives and with neither tools nor hope for moving forward. We're thrown back to our earliest days and get insights that inform the situations we are in now. We're reminded of how quickly we could become a newcomer again if we quit working our program—that is, if we survived the next relapse.

I was struck by how pretty Beth was when I first met her. She wore thick eyeliner around those big, beautiful eyes. I was impressed by the way she could cry big alligator tears without ever smudging her makeup. I used to tease her about that and make her laugh. She had a beautiful laugh.

Her baby never stopped crying. At first, I walked her out of meetings and into the hallway, offered to take the baby so she could go back in. She would refuse and begin to cry about how she loved this baby, but he was getting in the way of everything. All she wanted to do was get sober, but the baby made everyone hate her. She wouldn't let me take the baby so she could go back in the meeting. It wasn't the baby she was clinging to. She was caught on that razor edge between using and sobriety, where the slightest examination of your life floods you with more pain and shame than you think you can stand, while using offers the sweet promise of relief.

Although Beth attended many meetings, she always had the same "problem." Focusing on her baby enabled her to be there without actually being there. The other women were frustrated. Why couldn't she see how the solution to her crying baby was so straightforward? Because she couldn't. We could support her, tell her we had experienced this, too. But none of us, probably not even Beth, knew the depths of trauma, self-loathing and rage waiting to be unleashed if she put her baby down and looked into her own wounded heart.

She appeared and disappeared. It seemed Beth was doomed to be a newcomer forever. She went through sponsor after sponsor, each of them devastated when she relapsed. She would get a job, have a panic attack at work, do something outrageous, get fired, and then get high instead of calling her sponsor. She would fall in love with someone she met at a meeting. (Relapsing together is so romantic and such a familiar mistake.) Meanwhile, her baby grew into an adorable toddler whom we all loved.

Beth was killed in a car wreck far away from all of us who loved her. She had skipped town with a man, leaving her baby behind. There were no drugs or alcohol in her system when she died. We were left mostly with unanswered questions. We were lucky to have even found out at all. Deaths like Beth's are so hard on us who care.

After I had been a volunteer receptionist at this center for several months, the Director called me into his office. I was pretty scared of the Director and was certain he was about to tell me to take all my drama somewhere else and ban me from the center. I felt the panic rising, considered bolting out the front door to escape the humiliation of everyone in the center watching me be informed of all the reasons why I was unfit to work there, or anywhere. I imagined all the terrible stories people had been telling him about me to bring things to this point. In his office, I sat across from him, head averted, crippled with anxiety, waiting for the blow to land, just wanting to get it over with and be gone.

He offered me a job, a paying job, as the center's receptionist. I hadn't had a respectable paying job since I was a private investigator! What if I had run away from that center in fear when the Director asked to talk with me?

In my therapist's office, we discuss my secrets, the ones that are so deep and dark I sometimes can't even tell them to myself. She thought I might find it interesting to figure out why or how I could be so wrong about something like that conversation with the Director.

One of my first assignments on my new job was to email the minutes of a meeting to a group of people. "If you can't figure it out," the Director said, "just ask."

I couldn't figure it out. Sometimes you used the keyboard and sometimes you used the mouse. When I touched either, windows popped open and disappeared unpredictably. I would type, but no letters would appear. Other people used the computer with ease. It was the kind of thing anybody could do. There was no way I was going to show my ignorance and humiliate myself by asking. I avoided sitting in the receptionist's chair where that computer loomed over the desk and waited to get fired.

With my therapist's help I came to see that any man who had the slightest authority over me instantly turned into Daddy in my mind. If I thought he was in a bad mood, he might slap me upside the head. If he was acting kind, I knew a gentle explanation of why I was *worthless* was coming. Anything I said might make him blow up. What if my tone of voice was wrong when I said, "Good morning?" All the Director had done was ask me to do something I didn't know how to do. He even encouraged me to ask for help. I reacted as if it was a setup.

The Director was probably used to people like me. I did find someone willing to sit beside me, explain what was on the screen, and show me how and where to click until I learned how to send an email with an attachment. I wish I could say that all my Daddy issues melted away after that. What I can say is that I have another tool in my kit. When I'm consumed with the anxiety of knowing some man is about to publicly harm or humiliate me, I must ask myself, "Am I having a little visit from Daddy?"

I sit with my sponsor. We work the steps over this, starting with the first one. *What is it that has such power over me in these moments?*

Years of abstaining from drugs and alcohol didn't keep me from relapsing into my relationship addiction again and again. I found myself in another relationship where once more I felt unfairly treated by my partner. My therapist was listening to me try to sort out what I could and couldn't control. Although we weren't legally married, we did have a commitment ceremony at my church.

"I can't leave him," I told her. "I promised God that I would not flee the relationship because it was difficult. I would stay until I learned what I needed learn so the relationship would succeed. I'm not going to break that promise."

"How about we focus on some promises you can make to yourself?" she asked.

I made three promises that day. I would get my own cell phone so he couldn't screen my calls anymore. I would buy a CD player and some CDs so I could listen to music and sing again, even though that was forbidden. The next time I felt like I should leave, I would not make excuses to stay. I would simply go.

I did get my own phone and my own music. He was dumbfounded, and it made me a little bit afraid of him.

Soon there was an issue we needed to discuss. He wouldn't say a word. I tried everything to get him to talk. He acted like I wasn't even there. This is an enormous button-pusher for me. I watched myself raise my voice and yell, working my way to start screaming. He seemed to enjoy it. Time stopped. Was I really going to let this person have such power over me?

I arranged to spend the night with a girlfriend. At the center the next day I would be able to organize a new place for myself to live. Another friend came and helped me pack up my things. The soon-to-be-ex actually helped load my car, trying not to look bad in front of my friend, I figured. I packed what would fit and said goodbye to the rest.

There was a moment when we were left alone in the living room, and he took the opportunity to tell me he knew I'd already lined up my next man. That was so wrong, so far away from the reasons I was leaving.

I felt the surge in my chest, the desire to holler at him that he understood nothing.

Quietly, I exhaled long and slow. "You do not even know me," I said, and walked out the door. I didn't feel angry. I felt done.

That was the end of my last relapse, my last tumble into a relationship for no reason other than it was a relationship. Or rather, I want it to be my last relapse. If I don't keep working my program, it won't be.

Relationships—or all the promises that they hold—are truly my primary addiction. There is no high that I crave more than the sensation of falling in love, of floating on the delicious cusp of disappearing into someone's protection and care. You might say that I must never give up on love. There are healthy men out there. Someday I might meet The One. Keep your heart open, you might want to tell me.

You might as well tell an alcoholic that this new kind of beer is "refreshing" and won't get them drunk.

If I catch someone's eye or share a private joke, it can be like putting a match to my old junkpile of longing. Oh, it burns hot! I'm good at telling myself complicated stories. This time I am ready. This one will work because we started out as friends. Oh, the expectation! Oh the hormones! I can tell from the way they look at me that they are seeing directly into my heart with compassion and understanding. At last. God has sent him to me when I least expected it. Fairy dust obliterates my ability to do logic or remember patterns from the past.

If I keep responding to my craving for romantic love, I will die. God's love is the only all-encompassing love that is safe for me.

7. The City of Contentment

My therapist tapped a rhythm on my knees and asked me to visualize my emotions after ending my relationship so abruptly. With my eyes closed, I pictured myself at the edge of a perilous cliff, looking down. There was no bottom. The void threatened to rise up and claim me. I turned from the danger and walked away, but made no progress. An elastic band wrapped around my waist was pulling me back toward the cliff. It was thick and strong, the color of bubble gum, and shrinking, dragging me backward to my doom. Every time I took a step or two forward, it yanked me back. The struggle seemed futile, but I kept on straining.

Ahead was the skyline of a golden city, beautiful and welcoming. My therapist asked what the place was called, and I immediately knew its name. The City of Contentment. The place I had always strived to be. I struggled, more determined than ever to reach that city, where the grip and damage of the past would no longer be able to suck me back over that cliff of doom.

People showed up to watch. Despite the struggle, I sensed possibility. The people cheered and shouted encouragement. I made progress. I felt myself arrive and began to sing. All the people joined in. My Higher Power sang, too.

Here in the City of Contentment I am not free of my addictions, but I am disentangled from their deadly grip. I wake before dawn, make coffee, do my dishes, and sit at my desk. I read my daily devotions. I sing as much as my neighbors can stand. I bask in the presence of God.

Here, in the City of Contentment, I have liver cancer. The news hit me like a physical blow. My past was right back up in my face again. I thought of the massive damage substance abuse does to your liver. I remembered the needles, and the years I was afflicted with Hepatitis C. Did I really think I was going to escape unscathed? I observed myself starting up a world class pity-and-blame party.

Right there in the doctor's office, I looked up into the corner of the room, seeking the presence of God.

"Well, we sure have been through a lot, you and me," I told Him. "I'm tired. I have no fight left. You're going to have to be the one in charge of this battle. I'm giving it to you. All of it. The fear, the worry, the regrets, the blame. I'm going wherever you take me. You don't owe me anything. I already owe you my life."

Peace flooded over me.

The City of Contentment is filled with beautiful music. When I am singing, there is no room for pain. At church, they allow me to sing up front. I feel God's presence and sing without fear or performance anxiety. I look out at the congregation and they are all singing, too. We participate in the same presence. My heart floods with goodness and light. This is what people mean when they speak of "the glory of God."

Here in the City of Contentment, gratitude fills me. I was given 22 more years of life after I tried to kill myself. My notebook doesn't have enough pages to list the names of all the people who have brought me to this point. Catsup bottles continue to deliver exactly the right amount to just the right spot.

Here in the City of Contentment, I have a relationship with only one of my children. She goes with me to doctor's appointments when she can. Another daughter who doesn't speak to me has allowed me to view her Facebook page so I can see pictures of my grandchildren. I see the faces of my children in their faces. At my church, a small crowd of children thunders towards me after each service, calling me Grandma. Their earnest, tender faces shine with innocence and joy. Some of them are shy. My heart opens and we have a love-fest. I listen to their stories and heal myself by talking to them the way I wish someone would have talked to me.

Here in the City of Contentment, my connection to my church nourishes me. Nobody rolls their eyes at my "God talk." We pray together, share insights and encouragement, plan activities, and sing. So much singing.

Here in the City of Contentment, Jeremy is never far from my mind. I have so many happy memories of him, but every memory is tainted with some detail of my enormous failures. All memories lead to his last moments and my questions about what happened to him next. Is he trapped in that empty place of black tar unable to move or scream the same way I was when I tried to kill to myself? Did his suffering ever stop, or is he suffering still? These painful thoughts neither help me nor change anything. Again and again, I must give them to God.

Here in the City of Contentment, I am connected to mental health and recovery groups. I facilitate meetings for people with PTSD and anxiety. Every week I attend Co-dependents Anonymous for people with relationship addictions.

Here in the City of Contentment, pain does not take precedence. When I am flooded with rage over the cruelties others have inflicted upon me, I call on the example of Jesus who bore suffering and betrayals with dignity and grace.

In the City of Contentment, I am safe. I dwell in the peace I have sought all my life. I did not find peace, nor did it find me. The peace that I felt as a child in the presence of God and angels, cuddling my beloved SnoBall, is a sanctuary within me. After all those years of believing that peace was out of my reach, I now understand that dwelling in peace is a choice that I can make by choosing to dwell in the presence of God.

Acknowledgements

I am grateful to everyone who made this book possible, which is to say, everyone who has touched my life, especially Suzy Pennell, Terry Graff, my family, my children, their fathers, and the many people who guided my children into adulthood.

I honor all the addicts, girls on the stroll, cell mates, dealers, pimps, and dates who crossed my path. I never knew many of your names and today don't know if you are dead or alive. We taught each other terrible lessons. We had so much to learn.

I offer my humblest gratitude to people who have believed in me, despite what they know about me. Friends and supporters in rehab, meetings, and groups, especially Cathy Beckely, August Mae Walker, Darrell Keim, and Amanda Two-Spirits.

I am grateful for all the support that comes so generously from my community, especially members of the Garfield Christian Fellowship and the Garfield Community Church who are right beside me as I accept cancer into my life, They check on me, listen to me, drive me to doctors' appointments and welcome me into the warm circle of their families.

Many thanks to the people who helped me turn my experience into this book: Julie Reynolds who suggested it, Nancy Casey who carried it out, Adam Jones for assistance with technology, and Dan Crisman who helped me make a final review of the manuscript.

I would not be alive today if it weren't for my sponsors, the ones who endured the devastation of my many relapses, and the one I have today who is always ready to talk, day or night, to prevent another relapse. I thank my sponsees for their insights and for teaching me compassion, both for them and for myself. I pray for all those who have relapsed or disappeared.

My deepest gratitude is to God, my Higher Power. The God who raised me by revealing Himself, sending angels, and comforting me when I was a child who had no one. The God who loves me and sees me as worthwhile despite all the vile things I have done. The God who absorbs all my pain and envelops me in peace.

--Patricia Clayton

Author's Note

My role in this endeavor has been to write the book that Trish was unable to write because of her health.

Particular thanks to early readers who offered valuable comments. They include Martha Stroh, Wendy Norbum, M. Maxx Clark, and Jenna Wildeman.

--Nancy Casey

Patricia Clayton lives in Palouse, Washington with her service dog Daphne. She is active in groups that support mental health and addiction recovery in Washington and Idaho.

Nancy Casey is a writer, editor and teacher who lives near Moscow, Idaho. She is the author of *All the Way to Second Street*, a memoir of the back-to-the-land movement.